KITCHEN STEWARDING
Operation and Management

KITCHEN STEWARDING
Operation and Management

Dr. GULSHAN SONI

Ph.D. Hotel Management & Tourism Studies (U.S.A.)
M.Phil Tourism Management,
Executive MBA, MSci HM & CT,
Diploma in Training & Development, (M.H.R.D.)
G.H.O.T.P (J.P. Hotels Ltd.)

KANISHKA PUBLISHERS, DISTRIBUTORS
NEW DELHI-110 002

KANISHKA PUBLISHERS, DISTRIBUTORS
4697/5-21 A, Ansari Road, Daryaganj
New Delhi-110 002
Phones : 2327 0497, 2328 8285
Fax : 011-2328 8285
E-mail: kanishka_publishing@yahoo.co.in

Kitchen Stewarding:
Operation and Management

First Published 2011

ISBN 978-81-8457-250-6

PRINTED IN INDIA

Published by Madan Sachdeva for Kanishka Publishers, Distributors, 4697/5-21A, Ansari Road, Daryaganj, New Delhi-110 002, Typeset by Sunshine Graphics, Delhi, and Printed at Rajdhani Printers, Delhi.

Preface

The aim of this book is to cover the less explored but highly Poigant department of hotel industry. This book cover the basic as well as the advance kitchen stewarding management knowledge necessary for those involved in hotel industry at different levels. It is mainly cover the operation of kitchen stewarding department and their standard operation procedure, which has been developed with the help of a few Kitchen Stewarding Managers working in different five star hotels in India.

It covers all operations, equipment and material required by food and beverage department and, also cover the hygiene and sanitation according to HACCP, how this department helps in fulfill the standard of HACCP.

The inspiration to write this book come from the hospitality industry itself, as no such book on this subject is available. This book will not fascinate the professional but will also be perfectly suited to those who just starting their career in hospitality world.

Dr. Gulshan Soni

Contents

CHAPTER

1

Introduction to Kitchen Stewarding

OBJECTIVE OF THIS CHAPTER

- Introduction
- Layout of Kitchen Stewarding Area
- Organization Structure of Large Hotel
- Organization Chart of Small Hotel
- Duties and Responsibilities

Figure–Show the Cleaning of Plate by Utility Worker

In five star hotels, the kitchen stewarding department undertakes the primary duties of cleaning the back area of the restaurant and the overall kitchen premises along with the kitchen equipments like: deep fat fryers, girdles, hot plates, mixers, blenders, working tables and the like. If any of the heavy equipments are out of order, then the maintenance section of the engineering department comes in action. The stewarding function of a hotel kitchen is essentially charged to maintain and preserve the cleanliness and condition of the china, silver, glassware, equipment and working area of the kitchen:

- It is the department concerned with hygiene upkeep of kitchen equipments and their inventory.
- It Cleanliness the disinfects, stores, and regulate flow of equipments.
- It is a 24 hour operating department in any five star hotel.
- It work hand in hand with the food and beverage (service) and food and beverage (production).
- This department is also responsible for polishing of cutlery or electro plating of silverware.

All equipment large or small, heavy or light, requires ease in handling in order.

Figure–Show the Cleaning of Dishwasher by Utility Worker

To extend its life to maximum, minimize depreciation and maintain it in a reasonably attractive and efficient condition while in use. In small catering establishments the care and maintenance is generally entrusted to those who operate the equipment, in large establishments where heavy duty equipment predominates, a maintenance department perform this function.

In doing so the steward department maintains inventories and supplies of all equipment, china and silver and further, scrubs and cleanliness of all the working surfaces and floors of the entire kitchen. Also the care of the employee's cafeteria is the charge of the steward department. This section is thus responsible for:

- Storage and issue of cutlery, cookery, hallow are to the kitchen and restaurant.
- Cleaning and washing of above items and routine maintenance of all kitchen equipment, silver plating of cutlery etc.

The kitchen stewarding also disposes the garbage from the kitchen areas this working towards hygiene and cleanliness, overall it does the pot washing, dish washing and other cleaning duties to be performed it also take care of staff cafeteria.

So, it would not possible for a smooth operation in the kitchen or in an food and beverage service outlet without the kitchen stewarding active role.

This department is also responsible for polishing of cutlery or electro plating of silverware.

Garbage disposal and kitchen sanitation. Large deluxe hotel may require a large team for machine operation, banquet, night staff etc. figure show the organizational chart of the stewarding.

Duties and Responsibilities

Executive Kitchen Steward

He is responsible for all silver, dish and glass washing and the maintenance of high standards of kitchen cleanliness. He reports directly to the Executive Chef.

He should be familiar with all kitchen and service equipment, their usage, procurement, maintenance and storage, government laws enforced by health and sanitation department. His duties and responsibilities include:

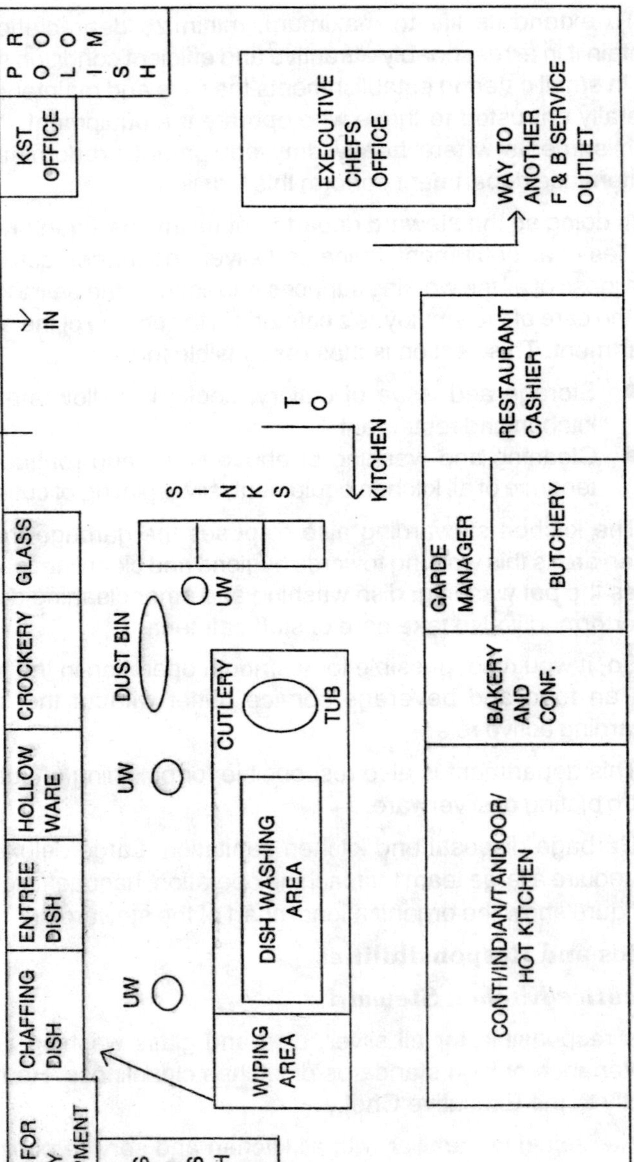

Figure-Show the Layout of Kitchen Stewarding to Part

Organization Structure

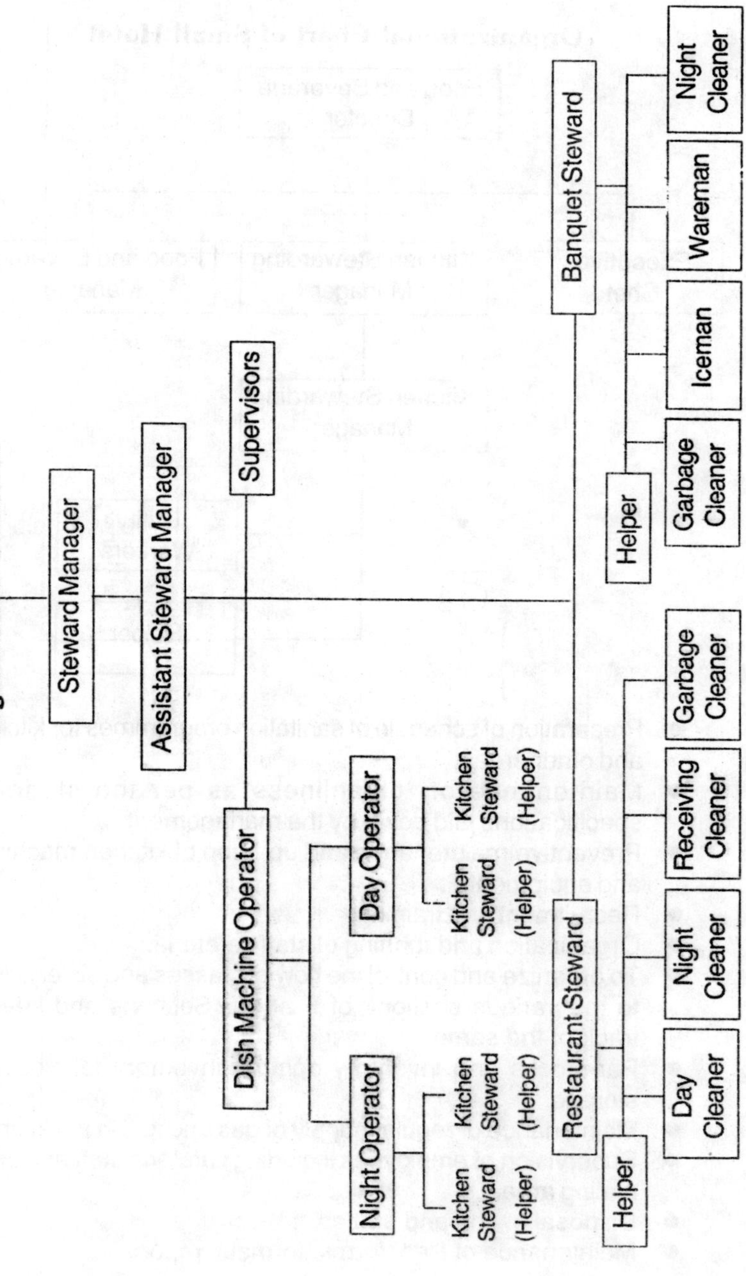

Organizational Chart of Small Hotel

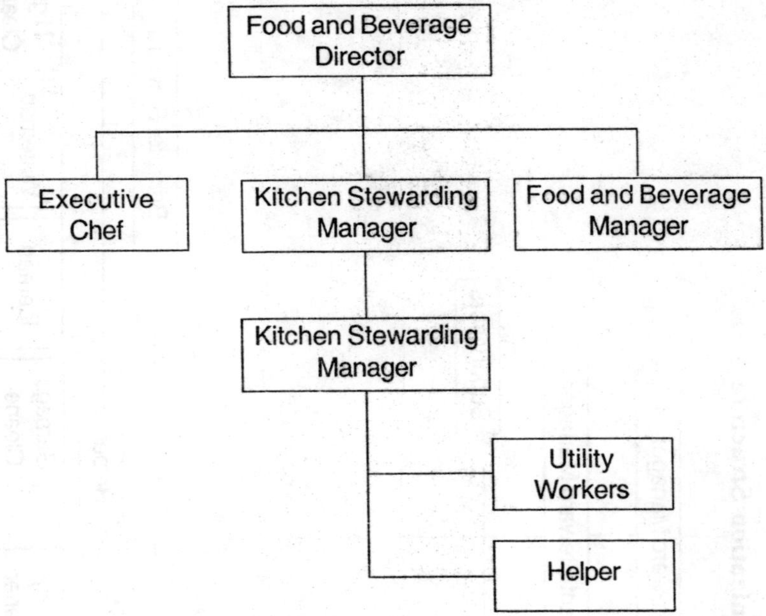

- Preparation of schedule of sanitation programmes for kitchen and other areas.
- Maintenance of cleanliness as per the standard specifications laid down by the management.
- Preventive maintenance and up-keep of kitchen machines and equipment.
- Recruitment and training.
- Organization and running of staff cafeteria.
- To organize and control the flow of glasses and silverware – to the various sections of F and B Sections and keep a track of the same.
- Par-stocks and inventory control, inventory takings and storage.
- Maintenance of regular supply of gas and fuel in the kitchen.
- Supervision of employees including cafeteria staff and silver plating area.
- Disposal of tins and bottles.
- Maintenance of files, forms, formats, reports.

- Annual six-monthly and quarterly forecast of expendable. equipment required for F and B Sections.
- Inter–departmental liaison.
- Liaison with municipal corporation.
- The kitchen stewarding department is headed by the manager.
- He directs the supervisor towards the task to be performed.
- Co-ordinates with the executive chef and manager.
- Responsible for cleanliness of the kitchen premises and supervises all the operations.
- Supervises purchase and requisition of the equipments.
- Maintain coordination with other departments.

Assistant Manager (Stewarding)/Head Stewards/Senior Supervisor

He assists the Executive Kitchen Stewards. He supervises utility personnel in the absence of the Chief Steward. He is a working supervisor and normally collects, bus carts, room service trays and cafeteria dishes. He scraps and stacks dishes and racks up glasses. He also makes the coffee, fills up ice trucks, rakes ice and mops lp spilled fluids. He distributes clean silverware in their proper storage areas.

- He comes in contact with the staff directly and daily.
- They follow the instructions of the kitchen stewarding manager.
- Divide the work equally among subordinates-i.e. utility worker he also gives allocations to the utility workers on any particular shift. For e.g., Raman to coffee shop kitchen, Shayam to main kitchen, Bharat to Chinese kitchen, and Rahul in banquet kitchen.
- He prepares the duty roaster and performance appraisal in consultation with the manager stewarding.
- Prepares inventory of all equipment.
- Trains the staff and gives incentives to improve their efficiency.

Dishwashers

Their Duties are:

- To clear and feed the stacked dishes into dish machine.
- To pull washed and dried dishes from the machine and stack them into carts.
- To run the glasses and silver utensils through the glass machines.

- Reports to kitchen stewarding supervisor.
- Clean and maintenance of pots, pans crockery and cutlery.
- Schedule chemical cleaning of silverware.
- Operating dish washing machine, maintenance, water refilling, cleaning agent refilling.
- Cleaning gas range, cold room, kitchen floors, working tables.
- Involved in physical count of food and beverage equipments under supervisor and manager.
- Collection of stores.
- Arranging kitchen area for operation like arranging entrée dishes, plates platters on kitchen counter.

Potman/Potwasher

He cleans all pots used by kitchen and soup kettles. During slack periods, he empties the kitchen garbage.

- Reports to kitchen stewarding supervisor.
- Clean and maintenance of pots, pans crockery and cutlery.
- Schedule chemical cleaning of silverware.
- Operating dish washing machine, maintenance, water refilling, cleaning agent refilling.
- Cleaning gas range, cold room, kitchen floors, working tables.
- Involved in physical count of food and beverage equipments under supervisor and manager.
- Collection of stores.
- Arranging kitchen area for operation like arranging entrée dishes, plates platters on kitchen counter.

Silverware

He clears, polishes and burnishes all silver flatware and hollow-ware. During slack periods, he clears all copperware.

Scullery Man (Plongeur)

He is responsible for the wash up of metal kitchen vessels and implements. The kitchen scullery is known as the plunge and the scullery man as the plunger casserole.

Night Duty Steward

The peak work load occurs at different sections at different times during the work shift, therefore, the related steward in each section will pitch in and help each other out under the direction of the supervisor on duty. His main duties are:

Main Range

- To clean thoroughly all grilled plates, trough, grease traps, edges and corners.
- To clean with oven cleaner all oven and salamanders.
- To clean steam tables, steam table stands and shelves below steam tables.
- Clean dust strong below steam tables.
- Clean shelves above steam table.
- Scrub down duck board and scrub below them.

Soup Kitchen

- To Clean all pots, steam kettles, large steamers and electric pots.
- To Clean all fixtures and exposed pipes.
- To Clean all shelves and wipe all boxes and cans and arrange neatly.
- To remove items from shelves below all work tables and remove and scrub all grill shelves.
- To wipe and polish sinks and pots of all work tables.
- To scrub floor.
- To thoroughly clean can opener.

Butcher Shop

- To dismantle and clean thoroughly the meat saw.
- To clean and protect with light coating and grease the food chopper.
- To remove and clean drawers of fish box steam inside and below the fix box.
- To scrub with soap and very hot water all other working surfaces.
- To scrape and clean thoroughly the chopping block and steel table.
- To remove items below tables and scrub the lower shelves thoroughly.
- To wash wall shelves and work sink thoroughly.
- To wipe refrigerator door.
- To scrub floor.

Pantry

- To remove and scrub duck boards.
- To scrub top of all working tables.

- To scrubs all wall shelves and shelves in all front areas.
- To wipe down coffee urns.
- To remove items from below work tables and scrubs the shelves below the table.
- To wipe down drinks and stainless steel edgings.
- To scrub floors.

Front of Kitchen

- To scrub all stainless steel areas including shelves and egg machine.
- To thoroughly scrub floors.

Garbage

- All garbage cans can be emptied and steamed out and scrubbed both inside and out.
- Garbage rooms to be cleaned and floor to be thoroughly scrubbed.

Bake Shop

- To clean sinks all work areas, be low work tables.
- To clean stove and ovens, inside and out.
- To scrub floor.
- To clean and polish stainless steel surfaces.

Ice

- Ice is to be raked in the morning.
- All the ice troughs are to be filled in the morning.

Coordination is of great importance not only between the various service staff members but also between them and the kitchen. It requires proper layout of the kitchen, as would facilitate the systematic and easy pickup of food by the waiter/waitress. Pickup areas should be early defined. Entrance and exists should be paid out to establish a standard format for traffic flow. In many hotels, a buffer zone is provided between the service and preparation staff by having a side man, mostly the chef, who transmits all order to the cooks.

CHAPTER

2

Food and Beverage Equipment

OBJECTIVE OF THIS CHAPTER

- Food and Beverage Service Equipment Material and Classification
- Points While Purchasing Tablewares
- Stainless Steel Equipments
- Enumeration of Silverware
- Items of Specialist Equipments and their Use
- Miscellaneous Tablewares/Items
- Chinaware/Earthenware/Crockery
- Classifications of Catering Chinaware
- Glassware, Classification and its Types
- Enumeration of Glassware
- Kitchen Equipments and Tools
- Categories of Kitchen Equipments
- Safety Precaution of Handling Equipments and Tools

Food and Beverage Service Equipment Material

Service equipment includes furniture, glassware, crockery, flatware and line for all those items which are affects the standard quality and style of the restaurants. Several factors are kept in mind when they are chosen.

1. Size of the restaurant
2. Theme of the restaurant
3. Types of service
4. Types of customers
5. Maintenance of equipment
6. Duality of equipment
7. Cost of equipment
8. Storage of equipment
9. Flexibility of equipment
10. Fit to corporate standard of the organization
11. Maintenance of equipment

Service Equipment

TABLEWARE

Tableware includes the dishes, glassware, cutlery, and flatware eating utensils (knives, forks, and spoons) used to set a table for eating a meal. The nature, variety, and number of objects varies from culture to culture, and may vary from meal to meal as well. Tableware may be categorized as given in Figure. Tableware is a term recognized as embracing all items of flatware, cutlery and hollowware.

Flatware

Figure–Shows the Flatware Items

Flatware denotes all forms of spoon and fork. Flatware, especially that used by most people when they eat informally, is usually made of stainless steel. As shown in Figure.

Cutlery

Figure–Shows the Cutlery Items

Cutlery refers to knives and other cutting instruments.

Hollowware

Figure–Shows the Hollowware Items

Hollowware refers to table service items such as sugar bowls, creamers, coffee pots, teapots, soup tureens, hot food covers, water pitchers, platters, butter plates and other metal items excluding flatware and cutlery. As shown in Figure.

Points While Purchasing Tablewares

- The type of menu and service offered.
- The maximum and average seating capacity.
- The rush hour turnover.
- The washing up facilities and its turnover.

Silver

(i) The manufactures often quote 10,15, 20 year plate. This denotes the length of life a manufacturer may clean for their plate subject to fair or normal usage.

(ii) The length of life of silverware also depends.

(iii) The weight of silverware also important.

(iv) The terms A-1 plate differs with every manufacturer. So it has no significance what so ever.

(v) There are 3 standard grades of silver plate.
A. Full standard plate
B. Triple plate
C. Quadruple plate.

(vi) The British standard–BS–5577 has been introduced to ensure to such terms as A-1 and 20 years plates. This standard was introduced in 1978.

Inn silver–plated tableware two grades have been specified.

(a) Standard: for general use

(b) Restaurant: Thicker grade for restaurant use and marked with an "R"

The minimum thickness of silver plating quoted should give a life of at least 20 years depending on usage.

(vii) The hallmark on silver tells two things. The two symbols represent the standard of silver used.

(viii) Plain cutlery and flatware is more too popular than patterned of the sample reason that it is cheaper and easier to keep clean.

(ix) The best is knives with handles of hard soldered silver, nickel or good stainless steel (Handles are an important factor in cutlery).

(x) The "sane wood" handled stainless steel is very good since it is impervious to boiling water and will not crack or chip.

(xi) Sterling silver is the most expensive type of silver used only in a few high class hotels.

(xii) Plate of E.P.N.S. (Electro Plated Nickel Silver) is more commonly used nowadays.

Stainless Steel Equipment

(i) Stainless steel, flatware and cutlery are available in a variety of grades.

(ii) The higher price designs are usually incorporated with alloys of chromium (which makes the metal stainless) and nickel (which gives a line grain and luster).

(iii) Good British flatware and cutlery is made of 18/8 stainless steel.

18%	—	Chromium
8%	—	Nickel
74%	—	Steel

Stainless steel is finished by different degrees of polishing

(a) High polish–Finish

(b) Dull Polish–Finish

(c) A light gray matte, non-reflective finish

(iv) Stainless steel resists scratching far more than other metals and therefore is more hygienic

(v) In neither tarnishes nor stains.

Storage

(i) Cutlery and flatware should be stored in boxes or drawers for each specific item lined with baize cloth (*to prevent items sliding about and getting scratched and marked.)

(ii) Hollowware should be stored on shelves, which are labeled showing where the item should be stored.

(iii) All flatware, cutlery and hollowware should be stored in a room or cupboard which can be locked since they constitute a large part of capital.

(iv) Cutlery and flatware can be stored in cutlery trolleys.

Enumeration of Silverware

Flatware

S.No.	Spoons	Size	Use
1.	Soup spoon	7 inches	To drink soup
2.	Large spoon or table spoon	8½ inches	To eat main course
3.	Dessert spoon or all purpose spoon	7 inches	For eating dessert and all purpose
4.	Service spoon	10 inches	For serving
5.	Salt spoon	3 inches	To apply salt
6.	Mustard spoon	3½ inches	Used in mustard pot
7.	Jam spoon/Preserve spoon	10 inches	To apply jam or preserves
8.	Coffee spoon	4½ inches	To stir coffee
9.	Tea spoon	5½ inches	To stir tea
10.	Demitasse spoon	3 inches	To stir in demitasse cup
11.	Egg spoon	4 inches	To eat boiled egg from egg up
12.	Ice-cream spoon	5 inches	for ice cream
13.	Grape fruit spoon	5 inches	To eat grape fruit
14.	Parfait spoon	5 inches	used in bar for mixing
15.	Bar spoon	5 inches	Used in bar for mixing
16.	Sundae spoon	5 inches	To eat ice cream in a tall glass

Forks

S.No.	Fork	Size	Use
1.	Fish fork	7½ inches	To eat fish
2.	Large fork or joint fork	8 inches	for main dish
3.	Dessert fork/All purpose fork	7 inches	All purpose
4.	Serving fork	10 inches	For service
5.	Fruit fork	4 inches	To eat fruits
6.	Pickle fork		To take pickle from pickle pot
7.	Pastry fork/Tea fork	5 inches	To eat pastry
8.	Carving fork	Various sizes	for carving
9.	Oyster fork	2 pronged	To eat oyster
10.	Snail fork	2 pronged	To extract the snail from its shell

Cutleries

S.No.	Knife	Size	Use
1.	Caviar knife	7 inches	Has a short broad blade used for spreading caviar

Contd...

S.No.	Knife	Size	Use
2.	Fish knife	7½ inches	To eat fish
3.	Large/Join knife	8 inches	To eat main dishes
4.	All purpose/dessert/small knife	7 inches	All purpose
5.	Steak knife (serrated edge)	7½ inches	To eat steak
6.	Butter knife	Various size	To apply butter
7.	Fruit knife	7 inches	To cut fruits in fruit basket
8.	Cheese knife	7 inches	To serve cheese from cheese board
9.	Carving knife	Various sizes	for carving purpose

Items of Specialist Equipments and their Use

1.	Asparagus holder	Use to hold Asparagus spears when eating
2.	Pastry slicer or gateaux sheer	Sweet Trolley–for serving portions of gateaux
3.	Corn on the cob holders	Corn on the cob--to pierce each end
4.	Lobster pick	To extract the flesh from the lobster caw
5.	Nut crackers	Dessert–In fruit basket to crack nuts
6.	Grape scissors	To cut and hold a portion of grapes and rinse
7.	Snail tongs	Used to hold the snail
8.	Snail dish	Dish is round with two ears–having 6 indentations to hold a portion of 6 snails
9.	Stilton scoop	For service of stilton cheese
10.	Silver skewers	Kebabs used for attractive presentation
11.	Sugar tongs	To serve cube sugar

Miscellaneous Tablewares/Items

	Item	Use
1.	Use sauceboat with sauce ladle	Kitchen made sauces are served
2.	*(i)* Bread basket or bread boat	Indian breads and bread slice are served in it
	(ii) Bread tongs	To serve bread
3.	Soup tureen	To keep soup in bulk for buffet
4.	Soup ladle	To serve soup from soup tureen

Contd...

	Item	*Use*
5.	Coffee pot	To serve coffee
6.	Tea pot	Comes in 4 capacities *(a)* 28.4 Cl *(b)* 56.8 Cl *(c)* 85.2 Cl *(d)* 113.6 Cl
7.	Milk pot/creamer	To serve cream/milk
8.	Sugar bowl/sugar basin	Usually used for keeping cube sugar
9.	Sugar tongs	Required to serve cube sugar
10.	Ice bucket	Used to serve ice cubes or crushed ice
11.	Ice tongs	Required for service of ice cubes
12.	Asparagus tongs	To serve asparagus
13.	Bud vase/center piece	for keeping flower bud on table
14.	Candle stand	To hold candle
15.	Toast rack/toast boat	To serve toast in table
16.	Coaster/Glass mat	Use to keep any glass while serving
17.	Butter pat or butter dish	To serve butter in table
18.	Lemon press	To squeeze lemon
19.	Cheese scoop	To scoop cheese
20.	Straw holder	To keep straws in table
21.	Toothpick stand	To keep tooth pick
22.	Egg cup	To serve boiled egg
23.	Ashtray	To collect ash from cigarettes and cigars
24.	Pickle pot	To keep pickles
25.	Tea strainer	To strain when serving dust tea
26.	Slop basin	To keep the tea strainer
27.	Table	Used on top of the table
28.	Cruet set	To keep salt and pepper: *(i)* Salt pourer *(ii)* Pepper-sprinkler
29.	Finger bowls	To serve after food to clean guests fingers after eating
30.	Salad bowls	To serve salads in buffet usually: *(a)* Wood

Contd...

Item	*Use*
	(b) Plastic *(c)* Ceramic
31. Hors d oeuvre platter or ravier	To exhibit different varieties of hors d oeuvres in hors d oeuvre trolley
32. Hors d oeuvre Trolley	Used to carry many raviers exhibiting different Hors d oeuvres
33. Fruit basket	Dessert–to serve fruits
34. Decanter	Used to serve soda or tonic water or water
35. Bottle or tin or can opener	To open bottles, tins and cans
36. Solid fuel containers	Container used to burn solid fuel
37. Solid fuel	Used to keep the chafing dish hot in buffet
38. Chafing dish	Used to keep buffet food
39. Chaffing stand	Used to hold chafing dish
40. Flat dish or platter	To serve rice, dry items etc.
41. Entrée dish	To serve side dishes
42. Nut board	Used to crack nuts
43. Salvers	Used to carry glass and other table wares comes in three different sizes: *(i)* Small *(ii)* Medium *(iii)* Large
44. Trays	Used to take orders in room service mostly comes in 3 sizes. *(i)* Small *(ii)* Medium *(iii)* Large
45. Menus stand	To hold small menu card.
46. Table number holder	To hold table number
47. Drawing pins	Used to frill in buffet and for other purposes.
48. Water jugs	To serve water
49. Wine cooler or wine chiller	To chill wines, usually white and champagne

Contd...

	Item	Use
50.	Wine basket or wine cradle	To keep red wines
51.	Wine cock screw	Used to open corks in wines
52.	Cocktail shaker	To mix cocktails
53.	Swizzle stick/stirrer	To stir drinks
54.	Optic/Peg measure	To measure drinks. (2 measures) *(i)* Large–60 ml *(ii)* Small–30 ml
55.	Cigar cutter	Used to cut the cigar smoking and to draw more smoke
56.	Gueridon Trolley	For gueridon service, can also be used for flambé
57.	Pastry Trolley	To exhibit different pastries
58.	Cheese trolley	To exhibit different types of cheese served in the restaurant
59.	Wine Trolley	To show different wines available
60.	Flambé Trolley	For flambé service
61.	Humidor	Used to show the varieties of cigar available
62.	Cheese board	To exhibit different types of cheeses

Chinaware/Earthenware/Crockery

Introduction

An establishment generally uses one design and pattern of China, but when as establishment has a number of different food service areas it is easier from the control point of view to have a different design in each service area.

Points on Purchasing Chinaware

(i) Every item of crockery should have a complete cover of glaze to ensure a reasonable length of life.

(ii) China should have a rolled edge, which will give added reinforcement at the edge. This means chipping will only occur on the under-edge, which is not visible to the customer.

(iii) To be satisfactory the pattern should be under rather than

on top of the glaze. Patterns on top of the edge glaze will become weak and discolour patter under he glaze is more expensive but its life will be longer.

(iv) Some manufacturers stamp the date, month and year on the base of the item. From this the life of the China under normal usage can be determined more accurately.

Different Trade Marks of Earthenware

(a) Vitreous
(b) Vitrock
(c) Vitrex
(d) Vitresso
(e) Ironstone
(f) Vitrified

Of these verified ware is recognized to be the strongest that does not always mean that every caterer buys vitrified hotel ware as other factors apart from strength and economy have to be taken into account.

Two new forms of crockery has come to the market they are known as:

(i) Steelite
(ii) Micratex

(i) *Steelite:* Is a vitreous China has a high chip resistance, has heat retaining quality, low absorption level which minimizes the risk of internal contamination has ability of the glaze to withstand high temperatures and pressures comes in variety of shapes and patterns to suit most needs.

(ii) *Micratex:* Is a form of crockery where the body strength of the China has been reinforced by a technique employed in grinding the Centiliter say this is to make the arty Centiliter stronger without adding to the weight.

Classifications of Catering Chinaware

There are classifications of catering chinaware. They are:

1. Bonechina
2. Hotel Earthen Ware
3. Stone Ware
4. Porcelain

1. Bonechina

Very fine, Hard China that is very expensive, the decorations are to be found under the glaze only. It can be made to thicker specifications for Hotel use. The price of bone china is very expensive.

2. Hotel Earthen Ware

Produced in vast quantities in United Kingdom and is the cheapest and least desirable hotel ware. It is not however guaranteed to the British Standard 4034 as is satisfied hotel ware. The specification for B.S. 4034 demands that vitrified tableware be non-porous which is also a guarantee of its strength. This form of tableware is cheaper than bone china. Vitrified Earthenware is particularly economical where it is in continuous use 25 hrs a day has heavy handling with a high turnover where hygiene is particularly important for e.g. in Montessori cafeterias, hospitals.

Domestic weight earthenware is also available, but this is lighter and thinner than the hotel earthenware on vitrified hotel ware previously mentioned.

3. Stone Ware

This is a natural ceramic material traditionally made in United Kingdom and fixed at a very high temperature, about 120°C. It is shaped by traditionally hand crafting techniques so there is wide variety of shapes and furnishes available, from mat to high gloss glaze. It is non-porous and extremely desirable with high thermal and shock resistance the price is slightly higher than earthenware due to long life guarantee.

4. Porcelain

This is of a completely different composition with a semi-translucent body normally blue/gray and has a high resistance to chipping it is a fine earthenware. While, this transparent or semi-transparent was first made in China.

Storage of Chinaware

Should be stored at a convenient high for placing. Should be stored on shelves in piles of approximately two dozen. Any higher may result in toppling down. If possible china should be kept covered to prevent dust and germs settling on it.

CROCKERY OR CHINAWARE

1.	Soup Plate	9 Inches diameter
2.	Entrée Plate/Half Plate Dessert/ Sweet/Fish/Fruit Plate Dessert Plate will have a floral design	9 Inches diameter
3.	Meat/Dinner/Large/Main Plate Joint/Full/Game/Cover Plate	10 inches diameter
4.	Quarter/Side/Cheese/Small Plate Under/B.B. (Bread & Butter) Plate	7 inches diameter
5.	Cereal Plate	5 inches diameter
6.	Salad Plate	7½ inches diameter *(a)* Kidney shaped *(b)* De Shape *(c)* Crescent shape *(d)* Half Moon shape
7.	Tea cup	6 2/3 ounce capacity
8.	Coffee cup (or) Breakfast cup	8-10 ounce capacity
9.	Saucer	6 inches diameter
10.	Demitasse cup	3½ ounce
11.	Demitasse saucer	3½ inches diameter
12.	Soup cup	7½ ounce capacity
13.	Consommé cup	10 ounce capacity

Other Items of Chinaware

1. Salad Crescent
2. Hot Water Jugs
3. Milk Jugs
4. Cream Jugs
5. Coffee Pots
6. Sugar Basin/Sugar Pot
7. Butter Dishes/Butter Pat
8. Ash Trays
9. Bud Vase/Centre Piece
10. Egg Cups
11. Soup Bowl/Cup
12. Platter

Glassware

Introduction

Everyone knows about the wide variety of beverages available but stop to consider the many kinds of glasses required to hold them. That will no longer apply to you, because this section discusses different glass types and their uses. Where it comes to wine, the glass is chosen not only because it is traditional, but also because it allows the wine bouquet to be appreciated and helps to maintain the proper temperature of wine.

The raw materials used for glass are silica and soda ash and even broken glass pieces called culets can also be used in the making of glass lead is added to make the glass crystal Centiliter sear.

Points While Purchasing Glasses

- *(a)* It should be completely transparent.
- *(b)* Should be free of air bubbles.
- *(c)* It should not be chipped or cracked.
- *(d)* The rim of the glass should be curved and blunt.

Types and Sizes of Glassware

1. Glass also contributes to the appearance of the table and the overall attraction of the room. Most manufacturers now imply hotel glassware in standard sizes for convenience of ordering.
2. Glasses are measured in terms of Fluid ounces or Out or Centiliter.
3. The term "3 out sherry glass denotes that one is able to get 3 glasses from one gill or a quarter of a pint (14-20 centiliter).
4. A 6 2/3 ounce (18.93 centiliter) denotes that it holds 6 2/3 Oz or 18.93 centiliter or one third of a pint.
5. There are three types of glassware
   - *(a)* Plain glassware
   - *(b)* Cut glassware
   - *(c)* Coloured glassware for example:
     Moseley glass. With green stems to serve Moseley wines Brown steam for Hocks.
6. The tulip shaped glass for champagne is used more than saucer since it retains longer the sparkle and effervescence.
7. The stem is long is some wine glasses so that the heat of the hand does not affect the wine while drinking.

8. Some glasses have a slight in curving lip in order to hold the aroma and it should be large enough to hold the particular wine being tasted.

Storage

1. Glasses are normally stored in glass pantry.
2. It should be placed in single rows on paper lined shelves GLASS ROLLY, upside down to prevent dust settling in them.
3. You can also stack glasses in plastic coated wire racks made specifically of the purpose of stacking and storing them.
4. The racks are also convenient while transporting glasses.
5. Tumblers should not be stacked inside one another as this may result in heavy breakages and cause accident to staff.

Enumeration of Glassware

Glass	*Capacity*	*Use*
Water goblet	10 ounce	To drink water
Highball glass	8 ounce	To serve water/soft drinks
Red Wine Glass (Std)	7 ounce	To serve red wines
White Wine Glass (Std)	5½ ounce	To serve wine
German/Alsace	6, 8 ounce	To serve Alsace/German Wines
Centiliter Wine Glass	6 to 7 ounce	To serve French Wine
Hock Glass (Tulip shape) Rhine Wines		Amber stem/Germany
Port Wine Glass	4 to 5 ounce	To drink Portugal Wines
Sherry Wine Glass	3 to 4 Oz	Elgin/Thistle Shape to drink sherry
Beer Goblet	12 Oz	To drink Beer
Burgundy Balloon	10 Oz	To drink Fr. Burgundy Wines
Champagne Tulip	9 Oz	To drink Champagne
Champagne Flute	6–8 Oz	do
Champagne Saucer	6 Oz	do
Beer Mug/Dimple/Tankard	12 Oz	To drink Beer
Large Beer Glass	12 Oz	To drink large Beer
Pilsner Beer Glass		To drink Pilsner Beer
Footed–Pilsner Beer Glass		To drink Pilsner Beer
Brandy Balloon/Snifter/Inhaler	8 Oz	To drink Brandy

Contd...

Glass	*Capacity*	*Use*
Juice Glass/Pony Tumbler	5 Oz	To drink Juice (Usually used in Room Service/Welcome Drink)
Rolly Polly	9 Oz	To drink cocktails
Collins Glass	10 Oz	To drink soft drink and other drink
Ice Tea Glass	12 Oz	To drink Ice Tea
Tumbler	10 Oz	To drink Squash
Spirit Glass	8 Oz	All Spirit
Old-Fashioned Glass	9 Oz	
Parfait	14 Oz	Specially Mixed Drink
Worthington Glass	10-12 Oz	
Cocktail Glass	2-3 Oz	Drink Cocktails

Classification of Glass

There are four classification of glass:

1. Crystal
2. Cut
3. Blown
4. Pressed

1. *Crystal*–Is the most expensive and rarely used in hotel expect in very special circumstance.
2. *Cut*–Is only used for special occasions.
3. *Blown Glass*–Is becoming more rare these days as the art is dying.
4. *Pressed Glass*–Is cheap to manufacturer and can be of a variety of strengths so that hotel glass can be heavy to give durability.

Types of Glassware

Many standard patterns and sizes of glassware are available to serve each drink. Most glass drinking vessels are either tumblers, flat-bottomed glasses with no handle, foot, or stem; footed glasses, which have a bowl above a flat base, but no stem; or stemware, which have a bowl on a stem above a flat base. Neither a tumbler, footed, nor a stem, yard (beer) is a very tall, conical beer glass, with a round ball base, usually hung on the wall when empty.

Collins Glass

A Collins glass is a glass tumbler, holding 240 to 350 ml, used to serve a mixed drink, named after Tom Collins. This glass is somewhat narrower, and holds less than the similar highball glass. As shown in Figure.

Figure–Shows the Collins Glass

Figure–Shows the High Ball Glass

Figure–Shows the Shot Glass

Highball Glass

A highball glass is a glass tumbler, holding between 8 and 12 fluid ounces (240 to 350 ml), used to serve a mixed drink, or highball. This glass is taller than an Old-Fashioned glass, and shorter than a Collins glass. As shown in Figure.

Shot Glass/Tequila Glass

It is a small glass used for measuring or serving up to three ounces of liquor. Modern shot glass holds a thicker base and sides than the whiskey glass. As shown in Figure.

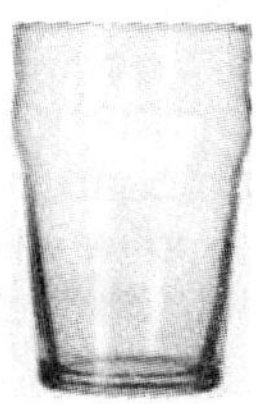

Figure–Shows the Pint Glass

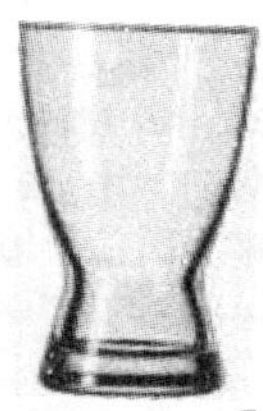

Figure–Shows the Pilsner Glass

Figure–Shows the Beer Tumbler

Pint Glass

A pint glass is a drinking vessel holding an imperial pint (568 ml) of liquid and is usually used for beer. Three common shapes of pint glass are found (conical, jug, and flared top), though others are available. Pints are considered good for serving stouts, porters and English ales. As shown in Figure.

Pilsner Glass

A pilsner glass is a glass used to serve many types of light beers, but is intended for its namesake, the pilsner. Pilsner glasses are generally smaller than a pint glass, usually in 250 ml or 330 ml sizes. They are tall, slender and tapered. Wheat beer glasses are often mistakenly referred to as pilsner glasses, but a true pilsner glass has an even taper without curvature. Pilsner glasses are made to showcase the colour, effervescence, and clarity of the pilsner, as well as to maintain a nice head. As shown in Figure.

Beer Tumbler

A beer stein is a traditionally-German beer tankard or mug, made of pewter, silver, wood, porcelain, earthenware or glass; usually with a hinged lid and levered thumb lift. As shown in Figure.

Figure–Shows the Flute Glass

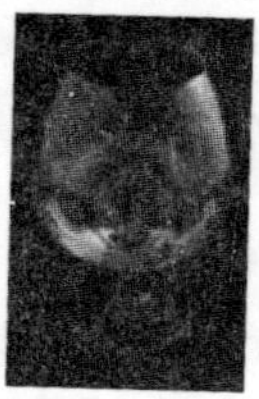

Figure–Shows the Sniffer Glass

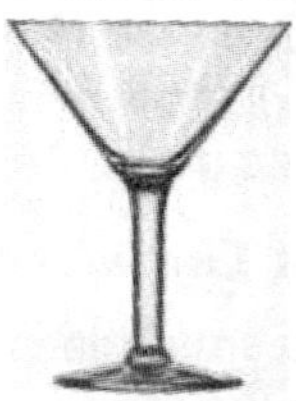

Figure–Shows the Cocktail Glass

Flute Glass

A flute glass is the preferred serving vessel for Belgian limbic and fruit beers. The narrow shape helps maintain carbonation, while providing a strong aromatic front. Flute glasses display the lively carbonation, sparkling colour, and soft lacing of this distinct style. As shown in Figure.

Snifters/Brandy Balloon

Typically used for serving brandy and cognac, a snifter is ideal for capturing the volatiles of aromatic beers, such as Belgian ales, India pale ales, barley wines and wheat wines. The shape helps trap the volatiles, while allowing swirling to agitate them and produce an intense aroma. As shown in Figure.

Cocktail Glass

A cocktail glass, martini glass, or champagne glass, or stem cocktail glass, is a drinking glass with a cone-shaped bowl (the tip of the cone forming approximately a 90 degree angle in the cross section) on a stem above a flat base, used to serve a cocktail or champagne. As with other stemware, the stem allows the drinker to hold the glass without affecting the temperature of the drink. One variation is the double martini glass which is taller and wider at the opening than a standard martini glass. As shown in Figure.

	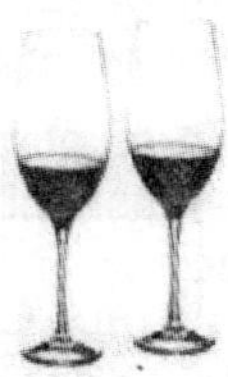	
Figure–Shows the Red Wine Glass	Figure–Shows the Bordeaux Wine Glass	Figure–Shows the Burgundy Wine Glass

Red Wine Glasses

Glasses for red wine are characterized by their rounder, wider bowl, which gives the wine a chance to breathe. Since most reds are meant to be consumed at room temperature, the wider bowl also allows the wine to cool more quickly after hand contact has warmed it. Red wine glasses (as shown in Figure) can have particular styles of their own, such as:

Bordeaux Glass

Tall with a wide bowl, and is designed for full bodied red wines like Cabernet and Merlot as it directs wine to the back of the mouth. As shown in Figure.

Burgundy Glass

Larger than the Bordeaux glass, it has a larger bowl to accumulate aromas of more delicate red wines such as Pinot Noir. This style of glass directs wine to the tip of the tongue. As shown in Figure.

White Wine Glass

White wine glasses are generally narrower, although not as narrow

Figure–Shows the White Wine Glass

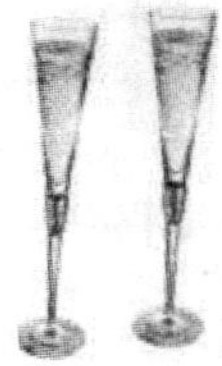

Figure–Shows the Champagne Flutes

as champagne flutes, with somewhat straight or tulip-shaped sides (as shown in Figure). The narrowness of the white wine glass allows the chilled wine to retain its temperature for two reasons;

- The reduced surface area of the glass (in comparison to red wine glasses) means less air circulating around the glass and warming the wine.
- The smaller bowl of the glass means less contact between the hand and the glass, and so body heat does not transfer as easily or as fast to the wine.

Champagne Flutes

Champagne flutes are characterized by a long stem with a tall, narrow bowl on top. The shape is designed to keep sparkling wine attractive and inviting during its consumption. The glass is designed to be held by the stem to help prevent the heat from the hand warming up the champagne (as shown in Figure) The bowl itself is designed in a manner to help retain the signature carbonation in the beverage. This is achieved by reducing the surface area at the opening of the bowl. Champagne flutes are often used at formal engagements, such as award ceremonies and weddings.

Some Important Points to Remember

1. Cocktail glasses are stemmed. Drinks served in cocktail glasses do not have ice in them–they are iced in the shaker-so the guest by holding the stem does not warm his drink with the heat of the hand sizes range from 7 to 17 Centiliter.
2. Highball glasses are those most commonly used in the bar. Long & straight sided they range from 14 Centiliter to 28 Centiliter, but 22 Centiliter in the most usual.
3. Collins glasses are tall and thin that range in size from 22 Centiliter to 37 Centiliter.

4. Sour glasses, for whisky sour etc., are footed and vary 11 Centiliter to 15 Centiliter but 11 Centiliter is the most common.
5. Water tumblers come in a variety of shapes–28 Centiliter and 30 Centiliter and are often used for soft drinks as well as water.
6. old fashioned glasses can be used for drinks actually know as 'old fashioned' and spirits served 'or the rocks' (with ice). They range in size from 14 Centiliter to 25 Centiliter and the mast common is 17 Centiliter.
7. Demonic glasses are straight side 11 Centiliter to 20 Centiliter.
8. Liqueur glasses are available in a variety of designs and shapes containing 2 or 3 Centiliter.
9. Pilsner–lager glasses hold approx 3 to 4 cm from bottom.
10. Beer tankard contain around 34 Centiliter.
11. Large cocktail glass–for a frappe or cocktail with crushed ice.
12. A sherry glass holding approximately 7 cm.
13. Vermouth glass (or wine or any aperitif served with out ice).
14. Sherry glass–alternative design.
15. Brandy Balloon–always the same shape to allow the brandy to release its aroma size vary.
16. Zombie or a long mix 28 to 30 Centiliter used to a variety of mixed drinks with ice & fruit.
17. Martini Jug or mixer–can come in a variety of shapes.
18. champagne saucer not the correct way to serve champagne but often used in hotels for quick service.
19. Punch Cup-used mostly at cocktail parties to serve punch-often hot, hence the handle like a cup.
20. Whisky or 'shot' glass for serving neat spirits i.e. without ice or mix.
21. Port wine glass holding about 7 cm.
22. Mixing or bar glass for stirred cocktails.
23. Long mix–same as 16.
24. Red wine glass approx 22 Centiliter. Wine should fill only half the glass, and tulip shape to hold the aroma.
25. White wine glass-about 17 Centiliter.
26. Decanter for water (served separately with whisky or a wine carafe).

Equipment and Tools

Kitchen equipment is expensive and to justify the expenses, it is essential that maximum use be made of it. This can be done only if the equipments work efficiently and this depends upon the care and maintenance. The type of fuel is to be used is an important factor. Though solid fuel and oil both have their place under certain circumstance, for professional cookery the choose lies between electricity and gas. The routine used, care and Centilitereaning of all items of equipment are important and this should be appreciated and understood.

When selecting equipment, capacity, trade name, good quality, simple design and easy to clean should be the criteria. The purpose and price is also considered.

Kitchen equipment may be dividing into various categories as given in Figure:

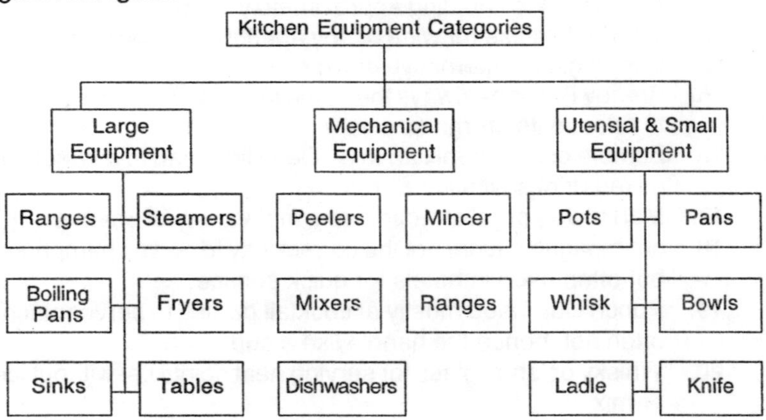

Figure–Shows the Various Categories of Kitchen Equipment

Equipments

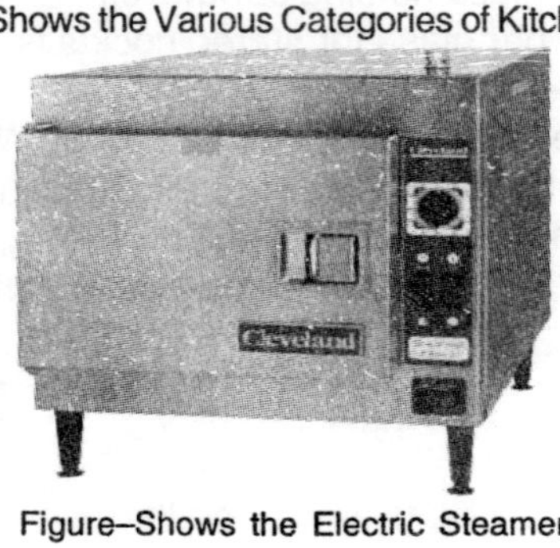

Figure–Shows the Electric Steamer

(a) Steamers

Steaming ovens that work from a main stream supply need little maintenance electric steamer shown in Figure. The door controls should be greased occasionally. The Steamers trays and runners should be washed in hot detergent water.

(b) Deep Fat Fryers

Modern fryers are heated by gas or electricity. Most incorporate a thermostatic control in order to save the fuel and prevent overheating. Deep fat fryer with two columns one for vegetables items to fry and one for non-vegetable items to fry as shown in Figure.

Figure–Shows the Deep Fryer with Two Columns

(c) Hot Cup Boards and Bain Marie

Hot cupboards are (commonly referred to in the trade as the hot plates) are used for heating plates and serving dishes and for keeping food hot. Care should be taken to see that the amount of heat fed into the hot cupboards and a thermostat is necessary in maintain this. An electric bain-marie as shown in Figure.

Figure–Shows the Bain Marie

(d) Grill and Salamander

Hot cupboards are (commonly referred to in the trade as the hot plates) are used for heating plates and serving dishes and for keeping food hot. Care should be taken to see that the amount of heat fed into the hot cupboards and a thermostat is necessary in maintain this. An electric bain-marie as shown in Figure.

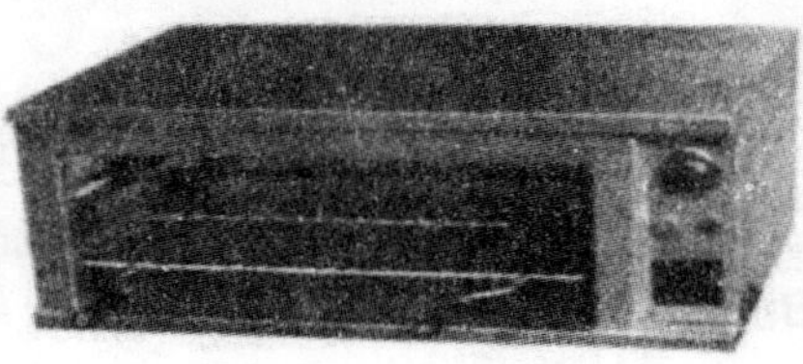

Figure–Shows the Salamander

The salamander, heated from above, probably cause more wastage of fuel than any other item of kitchen equipment, through being allowed to burn unnecessarily for long unused periods. Most salamanders have more than one set of heating elements or jets, and it is not necessary to have them all turned on.

Salamanders are heated by gas or electricity or a combination of the two. Electric type salamander as shown in Figure.

(e) Sinks

Different materials are used for sinks according to the purpose for which they are intended.

- Heavy galvanized iron pot wash.
- Stainless steel for general purpose.
- Glazed earthenware for general light purpose.

Figure–Shows the Stainless Steels Sinks

(f) Tables

Stainless steel tables are used in hotel industry, should be washed with hot detergent water, rinsed with hot water and dried. Stainless Steel table as shown in Figure.

Figure–Shows the Stainless Steel Table

(g) Potato Peelers

Potatoes should be free of earth stones before loading into the machine; otherwise damage to the machine will result. Before any potatoes are loaded, the water spray should be turned on and the abrasive plates set in motion. Different types of potatoes peeler are as shown in Figure.

Figure–Different Types of Potatoes Peeler

(h) Food Slicers and Choppers

Food slicers available are both manually and electrically operated. They are labour saving devices, which can be dangerous if not operated with care. Because, of this, the working instructions should be placed in a prominent position near the machine. Electric Food slicers are shown in Figure.

Figure–Shows the Electric Food Slicers

(i) Ranges

A range can be used to do almost any type of cooking. Ranges may be either gas or electricity operated. Gas range with oven and salamander as shown in Figure.

Figure–Shows Gas Range with Oven and Salamander

(j) Ovens

There are many types of oven. Range ovens have been traditionally and versatile piece of production equipment in most food service operations. Many ranges have ovens beneath them. Pan, steamer, oven, or warmer. Electric oven as shown in Figure.

Figure–Shows Electric Oven

(k) Tilting Braising Pans

A tilting braising pan is flat–bottomed and can be used as a kettle, griddle, fry pan, steamer, oven, or warmer/service. Electric Tilting pan as shown in Figure.

Figure–Shows the Electric Tilting Pan

Figure–Shows the Mixers

Mixers

A mixer is a kitchen appliance intended for mixing, folding, beating, and whipping food ingredients. Mixers come in two major variations, hand mixers and stand mixers. A hand mixer, as the name implies, is a handheld mixing device. It typically consists of a handle mounted over a large enclosure containing the motor, which drives one or two beaters. The beaters are immersed in the food to be mixed. A stand mixer is essentially the same as a hand mixer, but is mounted on a stand which bears the weight of the device. Stand mixers are larger and have more powerful motors than their handheld counterparts. They generally have a special bowl that is locked in place while the mixer is operating. Heavy duty commercial models can have bowl capacities in excess of 100 quarts (95 L). Typical home and commercial models are equipped with bowls of around 4 quarts (4 L). A typical home dick stand mixer will include a wire whip for whipping creams and egg whites; a flat beater for mixing batters; and a dough hook for kneading.

Blender

A blender or liquidizer is a kitchen appliance used to mix ingredients or puree food. The blending container can be made of glass, plastic, or stainless steel, and often has graduated markings for approximate measuring purposes. At the top of the container is a lid to prevent ingredients from escaping during operation. At the Bottom is a serrated blade assembly, sometimes removable for cleaning purposes.

Figure–Shows the Varieties of Blender

Refrigerators

A refrigerator (often called a "fridge" for short) is a cooling appliance comprising a thermally insulated compartment and a mechanism to transfer heat from it to the external environment, cooling the contents to a temperature below ambient. Refrigerators are extensively used to store foods which deteriorate at ambient temperatures; spoilage from bacterial growth and other processes is much slower at low temperatures. A device described as a "refrigerator" maintains a temperature a few degrees above the freezing point of water; a similar device which maintains a temperature below the freezing point of water is called a "freezer". Freezers keep their contents frozen. They are used both in households and for commercial use. Most freezers operate at around -18°C (0°F)

Figure–Shows the Three Door Refrigerator

UTENSILS AND SMALL EQUIPMENTS

Cookware and Bake Ware

Cookware and bake ware are types of food preparation containers commonly found in the kitchen. Cookware comprises cooking vessels, such as saucepans and frying pans, intended for use on a stove or range cook top. Bake ware comprises cooking vessels intended for use inside an oven. Some utensils are both cookware and bake ware.

Braising Pans and Roasting Pans

Braising pans (Also known as braisers and roasters) are large, wide and shallow, to provide space to cook a roast (chicken, beef, or pork). They typically have two loop or tab handles, and may have a cover. Roasters are usually made of heavy gauge metal so that they may be used safely on a cook top following:

Figure–Shows the Roasting Pans

Roasting in an oven. Unlike most other cooking vessels, roasters are usually oblong or oval. There is no sharp boundary between braisers and roasters-the same pan, with or without a cover, can be used for both functions.

Casserole Pans

Casseroles pan (for making casseroles) resemble roasters and dutch ovens, and many recipes can be used interchangeably between them. Depending on their material, casseroles can be used in the oven or on the stovetop. Casseroles are commonly made of glazed ceramics or Pyrex.

Figure–Shows the Casserole Pans

Figure–Shows the Dutch Ovens

Dutch Ovens

Are heavy, relatively deep pots with a heavy lid, designed to re-create oven conditions on the stovetop (or campfire). They can be used for stews, braised meats, soups, and a large variety of other dishes that benefit from low heat, slow cooking. Dutch ovens are typically made from cast iron, and are measured by Volume.

Large and Small Skillets

Frying pans, fry pans, or skillets provide a large flat heating surface and shallow sides, and are best for pan frying. Fry pans with a gentle, rolling slope are sometimes called omelets' pans. Grill pans are fry pans that are ribbed, to let fat drain away from the food being cooked. Fry pans and grill pans are generally measured by diameter (20–30 cm).

Figure–Shows Large and Small Skillets

Saucepans (or just "pots")

Are vessels with vertical sides about the same height as their diameter, used for simmering or boiling? Saucepans generally have one long handle. Larger pots of the same shape generally have two handles close to the sides of the pot (so they can be lifted with both hands), and are called sauce-pots or soup pots (3–12 litres). Saucepans and saucepots are measured by volume (usually 1–8 L). While saucepots often resemble dutch ovens in shape, they do not have the same heat conduction characteristics.

Figure–Shows the Saucepans

Sauté Pans

Sauté pans are used for sautéing, have a large surface area, like a fry pan, but with vertical sides, to prevent food from escaping during cooking.

Figure–Shows the Sauté Pans

Stockpots

Stockpots are large pots with sides at least as tall as their diameter. This allows stock to simmer for extended periods of time without reducing too much. Stockpots are typically measured in volume (6–36 L). Stockpots come in a large variety of sizes to meet any need from cooking for a family to preparing food for a banquet. A specific type of stockpot exists for lobsters, and an all-metal stockpot usually called a caldero is used in Hispanic cultures to make rice.

Figure–Shows the Different Varieties of Stockpots

Woks

Wok is typically lens-shaped. This allows a small pool of cooking oil to be heated to a high heat using relatively little fuel, while the outer areas of the wok are used to keep food warm after it has been fired in the oil. In the Western world, woks are typically used only for stir-frying, but they can actually be used for anything from steaming to deep frying.

Figure–Shows the Different Varieties of Wok

Baking Pans

Baking pans are designed for use in the oven (for baking) and encompass a variety of different styles of bake ware such as cake pans, pie pans, and loaf pans. These are often made from light or medium gauge metal. The longest lasting baking's sheets and pans are made with heavy-gauge steel or aluminium. They are heavier in weight which helps in heat distribution evenly and prevents the metal from warping.

Figure–Shows the Different Baking Trays

Cake Pans

Cake pans include square pans, round pans, and specialty pans such as angel food cake pans and spring form pans often used for baking cheesecake.

Figure–Shows Different Cake Pans

Cutting, Mashing, Grating and Grinding Tools

Cutting

Figure–Shows the Different Knifes

FROM TOP LEFT: cleaver, utility knives (next two), slicer, flexible slicer, scimitar, Serrated slicers (pointed and round-tipped)

FROM BOTTOM LEFT: French knives (first three in row),

Boning knife, granton-style edge French knife, paring knife, tourné knife

A chef's knife, also known as a French knife, is a cutting tool used in food preparation. It is the primary general-utility knife for most Western cooks. A chef's knife generally has a blade eight inches (20 cm) in length and 1 and a half inches in width, although individual models range from six to 14 inches (15 to 36 cm) in length.

Grater

Grater is a kitchen utensil used to grate foods into fine strips or crumbs. Several types of graters have different sizes of grating slots, and can therefore aid in the preparation of a variety of foods. They are commonly used to grate cheese and lemon or orange peel (to add zest), and can also be used to grate other soft foods. They are commonly used in the preparation of toasted cheese, welsh rarebit, and macaroni and cheese.

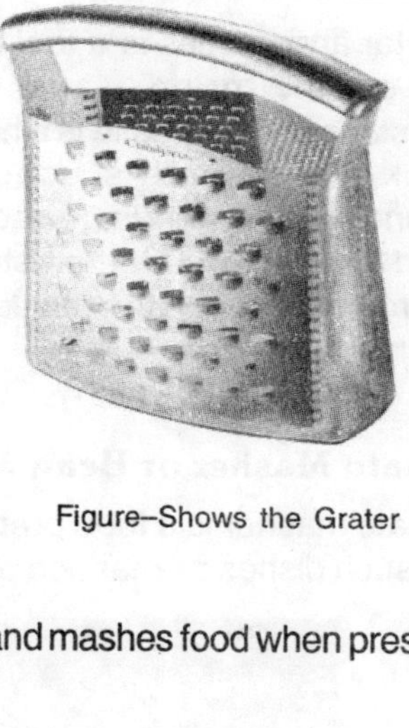

Figure–Shows the Grater

Chinois

Chinois fits on top of a deep container and mashes food when pressed through it.

Figure–Shows the Chinois

Eggbeater

Eggbeater used to beat mixture vigorously and homogenize.

Figure–Shows the Beater

Mortar and Pestle

Mortar and pestles is a tool used to crush, grind, and mix substances. The pestle is a heavy stick whose end is used for pounding and grinding, and the mortar is a bowl. The substance is ground between the pestle and the mortar.

Figure–Shows the Mortar and Pestle

Potato Masher or Bean Masher

Potato masher is a food preparation utensil used to crush soft food for such dishes as mashed potatoes, apple sauce, or refried beans.

Figure–Shows the Patato Masher

Meat Mallets

Meat mallets tenderize or flatten meat. Made from wood or metal, they are typically two-sided, one flat with slight bumps, and the other with more pronounced protrusions. Meat mallets can be made from wood, plastic, or steel, but their use has lessened with the invention of cube steak machines and other electric tenderizers. Meat mallets can also be used to crush ice.

Figure–Shows the Meat Mallet

Vegetable Peelers

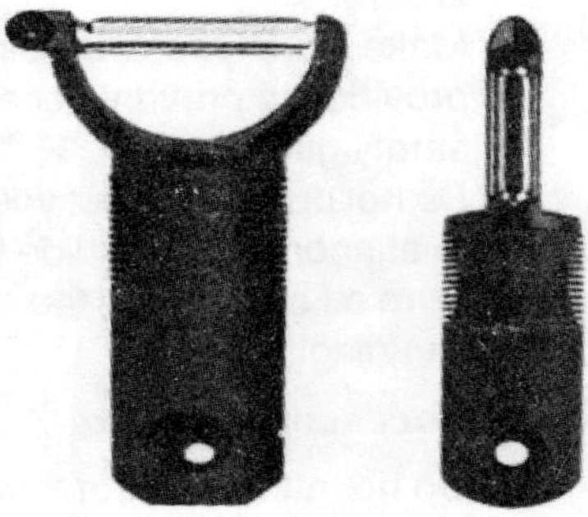

Figure–Shows the Vegetable Peeler

A peeler is a metal blade attachec to a metal, plastic or wooder handle that is used for peelinç vegetables, frequently potatoes There are two main varieties, the 'Yorkshire' (or sometimes callec a Lancashire peeler) desigr involving the blade as an extensior of a handle, in much the same way as the blade is attached to a knife. The second variety more closely resembles a safety razor (sometimes it is called a Y-peeler (due to its shape), rex peeler, yoke peeler, or speed peeler), with the blade perpendicular to the handle, is used with a similar action to a razor, shaving off skin in strips parallel to the handle. Most speed peelers have an 'eye gouger' beside the blade, a loop of metal used to dig out eyes and blemishes from the potato. Peelers can be used on citrus fruits, asparagus, eggplant, tomatoes and even mushrooms.

Safety Precaution of Handling Equipments and Tools

Before operating any machinery workers should:

- Get trained in their use.
- Wear any personal protective equipment provided by your employer.
- Use any machine guarding provided.

- Always ask for help if you are not sure how to do something.
- Be aware that age restrictions exist for workers under the age of 18 from using or cleaning certain equipment.
- Follow the manufacturer's instructions for machine use and cleaning.
- Follow the general recommendations below to identify and avoid potential hazards associated with kitchen machinery.

Mincers, Choppers, Dicers, Slicers

- Always use push sticks or tamps to feed or remove food from these types of machines.
- Do not use your hands to feed smaller pieces of meat through slicers.
- Make sure you are using any machine guarding that is provided to prevent access to cutter blades. Do not bypass safety guards.
- Do not open up or put your hands into an operating machine to stir contents or guide food.
- Turn off and unplug the machine before disassembling and cleaning.

Food Processors, Mixers

- Do not attempt to remove items (for example, a spoon that falls into the mixture) from dough while the machine is mixing.
- Do not open up the lids of processors to stir contents while food is processing.
- Make sure the processor is off before opening the lid or adding items.
- Turn off and unplug machinery before cleaning or removing a blockage.
- Use any machine guards provided.
- Do not wear loose clothing or jewelry that could become caught in machinery.

Microwaves

- Microwave ovens in poor repair may omit radiation.
- Make sure the microwave is located at approximately waist level and within easy reach, to provide for ease in the lifting of hot foods.
- Follow manufacturer's instructions for operating microwave ovens.

- Cover foods cooked in microwaves to avoid splattering.
- Use caution when opening tightly covered containers. Open containers away from your face because they may be under pressure and could be extremely hot.
- Use appropriate personal protective equipment such as hot pads when removing foods from microwave.
- Make sure door seals are in good condition and free from food or grease buildup.
- Do not use a microwave if it has a door that is damaged or doesn't lock properly. Damaged ovens may emit harmful radiation.
- Do not microwave metals, foil, or whole eggs.
- Keep the interior of the microwave clean to avoid splattering and popping.
- If you notice any sparking inside the microwave, immediately turn off the microwave, unplug it, report it to the supervisor, and do not use it.
- Be advised that microwaves may interfere with the workings of pacemakers.
- Be aware that food cooked in the microwave can remain hot long after the microwave turns off.

Steamers/Pressure Cookers

- Do not open the door while the steamer is on, shut off the steam, and then wait a couple of minutes before releasing the pressure and opening.
- Clear the area around the steamer before opening.
- Open the steamer door by standing to the side, keeping the door between you and the open steamer.
- Use oven mitts to remove hot trays from the steamer.
- Place hot, dripping steamer trays on a cart to transport. If trays are carried by hand, they will drip on floors and create a slip hazard.
- If a steamer is stacked, remove the tray from the top steamer first, then the lower one, to prevent burns from rising steam.

Pressure Cookers

- Shut off the steam supply and wait for the pressure to equalize before opening the lid of the pressure cooker.
- Stand to the side and open the pressure cooker away from

yourself, keeping the open lid between you and the pressure cooker.

Coffee Makers

- Do not place hot coffee makers close to the edge of counters where people passing by may come in contact with them.
- Check to make sure the coffee filter is in place before making any coffee.
- Do not remove the filter before the coffee has stopped dripping.
- Never stick your fingers into the chamber of a coffee grinder to get beans to drop into the grinder; tapping on the outside of the container will encourage beans to drop into grinder.

CHAPTER

3

Dishwashing

OBJECTIVE OF THIS CHAPTER

- Introduction
- Cleaning of Dishwashing Machine
- Common Ingredients Used
- The Dishwashing Process
- Guidelines of Efficient Dishwashing
- Dishwashing Units
- Pot or Pan Washing
- Cleaning Methods
- Schedule for Care of Equipment
- Normal Cleaning of Materials
- Detergents and its Actions
- Silver Room or Plate Room
- Silver Cleaning Methods

Introduction

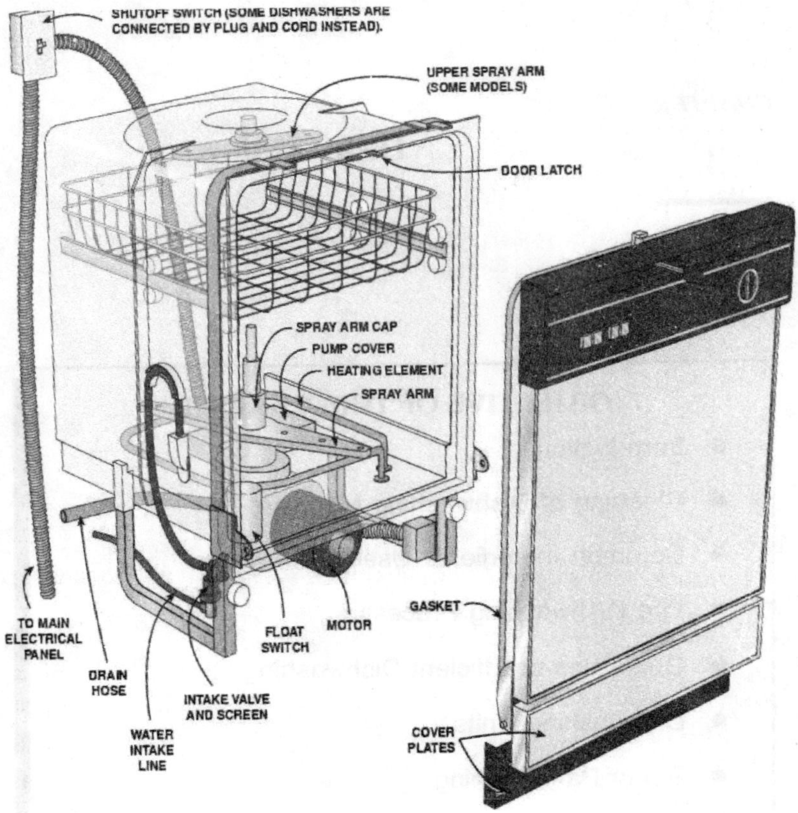

Figure–Shows the Inner Description of Dishwashing Unit

The common adherents are saliva, lip marks food particles of fat, protein and carbohydrate residues.

All cleaning involves the use of water a detergent or scouring powder or abrasive and something to scrub with, the nature of these components affect the quality of the wash.

Cleaning Dishwashing Machine

The dishwashing machine must be thoroughly cleaned after each use.

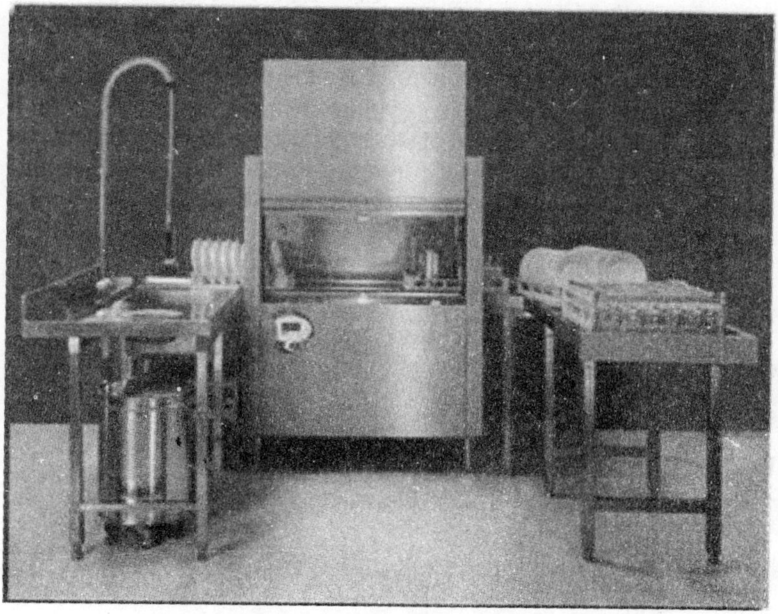

Figure–Shows the Dishwashing Machine Unit

The following procedures are to be followed:

- Turn off the switch.
- Secure the steam and hot water valves to the final rinse mixing valve or the steam and hot water valves to the hot water booster heater.
- Add ¾ to 1½ cups of dishwashing machine detergent to the rinse tank, depending on the capacity of the rinse tank.
- Turn the machine on and allow it to operate for 5 minutes.
- Turn the machine of and secure the steam valve to the rinse tank.
- Open the drain valve to the wash and rinse tanks: open the door and allow the machine to cool
- Remove the doors, scrap screens, metal frames, wash and rinse spray arms, pump intake strainer, drain strainer, and splash curtains. Wash thoroughly in the utensils wash sink and rinse.
- Using hand –dishwashing detergent and water with a nylon-bristled brush, thoroughly clean the inside and outside of

the machine rinse with clean water to remove all loosened dirt and detergent.

- Reassemble the machine, close the drain valve to the wash and rinse tanks.
- Fill the tanks half full of water, open the steam valve to the rinse tank and allow the temperature to reach 180°F.
- Turn the machine on and operate for 5 minutes without detergent.
- Turn the machine off, close the steam valve to the rinse tank, and open the drain valves to the wash and rinse tanks.

Note: Follow the same basic procedures for the single-tank dishwashing machine with the exception of steps 1 through 4.

Common Ingredients Used

Water

Two important aspects to consider

(i) Quality
(ii) Temperature. The quality refers to its being unpolluted and soft.

When calcium and magnesium ions are present in water it is known as "hard water" when such water repeatedly used for washing dishes, scales form on the equipment. This forms a coating which prevent effective heat transfer scaling may also block pipes by leaving deposits.

Degree of Hardness is used in Parts Per Million (PPM)

Soft water has better cleansing properties and foams better with soaps. It is also provides better penetration of detergents into the material adhering to dishes and removes them completely.

Water of high temperature in dishwashing helps to destroy micro-organisms besides softening the water. Temperature best suited are 50°C for pre rinse 60°C for the wash and 80°C for the final rinse.

Detergents

They are cleaning agents capable of something grease or foreign materials adhering to surfaces. The most common of less are soaps, in the form of powders or liquids acid cleaners, grease solvent and abrasives.

Alkalies are also added to some cheaper detergents because of their ability to form soaps with fat form the soiled surfaces. While these can take care of the dishes, alkalies detergents harder the water and therefore have poor rinsing qualities besides, alkalies exert a corrosive action on the dishes affecting their sheen and making surface rough. They are also harsh on the hands that wash the dishes.

A good detergent has the ingredients to soften hard water, dissolve out adherent and obstinate stains without having a corrosive action either on the dishes or on the hands.

Abrasives

A substance used with friction to rub off difficult stains from equipment, stain which do not get dissolved with water and non-corrosive detergents, such as those of animal and vegetable fats and carbon residues require abrasive or scouring powder. e.g.: silver sand, pumice powder, steel and glass woods. Red brick powder +tamarind is a good scourer for brass, in paste form scouring powders are gentler in their action both on equipment and hands.

The Dishwashing Process

Scraping waste from plates.
Equipment into bin →→ soaking dishes in hot water
↓
Washing out detergent ←← soaking in detergent water
↓
Rinsing in warm water
↓
Rinsing in hot water→→ stacking on racks for air drying
↓
Back for use

Guidelines of Efficient Dishwashing

- All plates waste, leftover and swill to be collected away from the dishwashing area in covered bins.
- Dishwashing is a continuous process to avoid areas which can become sources of contamination. No equipment to be collected to be washed at the end of service.
- Free flow hot water should be available.
- Knives and other sharp tools into the sinks.

- Utility staff or washing staff to be informed if a hot pan is placed on the drain board for washing.
- All cooking pans must be soaked immediately after use too loosen adherents and decrease washing efforts.
- Dishwashing staff to be equipped with non-ship gloves to protect hand from strong detergent and the heat of the water and avoid shipping.
- Handling of washed utensils should be minimized. This can be done if they are allowed to drain and air dry in their storage racks, to be removed only when required for use.
- All equipments should be dry before it is put away.

Dishwashing Units

Food service establishment which operate on traditional methods, the most suitable arrangement for dishwashing is to make provision for a row of three sinks, one each of pre washing, washing and rinsing. Small establishment can use a double sink arrangement for dishwashing, in which water is changed frequently while larger establishment used 3 to 5 sinks.

Washing by machines saves time and effort and increase safety, co2 temperature near boiling point can be used.

Types of Dishwashing Machines

These are four types of dishwashing machines:

- Single tank DWM (normal and rack type)- 75 per cent market share
- Multi–tank /conveyor DWM (20% Market Share)
- Dump (5% Market Share)
- Low Temperature DWM

PREPARATION FOR MWW

(Machine Ware Washing)

- Check filters, scrap trays water hardness
- Replace curtains
- Check wash jets
- Check product levels/concentration
- Close drain valves
- Fill machines

- Switch on heaters
- Switch on dosing pumps
- Check temperature
- Switch on machine

Basic Steps in Machine Ware Washing

These are eleven basic steps in Machine Ware Washing

1. Sorting of the crockery by size and type
2. Pre–scrap (using scourer if necessary)
3. Per–soaking of heavily soiled cutlery
4. Turn cups and glasses upside-down'
5. Mix cutlery handles downwards
6. Use the right baskets
7. Wash glasses separately
8. Pre–rinse separately
9. Main wash using detergent
   Wash tank 1 55-60°C
   Wash tank 2 60-65°C
10. Pressure Rinse (65-75°C)
11. Final Rinse (80-85°C)

Pot or Pan Washing

Includes the washing of food holding equipments from Bain-Marie or heated trolleys. Abrasive to be with selected care so that surface of pans are not scratched or chipped. Through cleaning teapots and coffee urns everyday with long handled hard brushes.

Cleaning Methods

All equipments large or small, heavy or light require care in handling. Use and storage in order to extend its life to the maximum, minimizes depreciation.

Schedule for Care of Equipment

- Keep all equipments clean.
- Wash all detachable parts of the equipment with suitable detergent and hot water after each use.
- All small equipments like cutlery, ladles, chopping board, kitchen tools should be washed after every use and placed in their concerned drawers.

- Check that all pieces are in working order.
- Repair must be attended without delay to prevent the equipment from being damaged and obstructing work for any period of time.
- A weekly fortnightly or monthly programmed for oiling and servicing the equipment should be followed.
- All electrical inputs to the equipment should be checked periodically to ensure that proper electrical load is available for efficient functioning.
- Assign the care of each machine to one responsible person.

Normal Cleaning of Materials

- *Metals:* as a rule, it should be cleaned immediately after use.
- *Marble:* scrub with a bristle brush and hot water and wipe dry.
- *Plastic:* wash in reasonable hot water and soap solutions.
- *Stainless Steel:* soak in hot detergent water. Clean with a scrubber or brush rinse and dry.
- *Abrasives:* it should be used only in moderation as their constant scratching of the surface makes it more difficult to clean the articles next time.
- *Copper:* scrape out as much food as possible.

Detergents

Detergent are products made up of a solvent; a wetting agents and water they are cleansing agents or substances capable of removing grease or foreign materials adhering to surfaces. The most common of them are shops, in the form of powders or liquids, acid cleansers, grease solvents and abrasives.

A good detergent has the ingredients to soften hard water, dissolve out adherents and obstinate stains without having a corrosive action either on the dishes on the dishes or on the hands. It is not always possible to find a detergent which is equally good for metal, china glass, wood and laminates, but a wide variety are marketed to choose from.

Action of Detergents

Detergent act in three phases:

- First, they penetrate the materials sticking to the dish, going between the particles of the adherents and the surface of the dish to be washed. This process helps to reduce the tension between the particles and the dish.

- Second, the particles of the detergent get suspended in the water or washing solution.
- Third, the detergent liquid should be removed by thorough rinsing of the dishes and the particles to leave dishes clean.

To ensure that all the detergent is rinsed away it is desirable to rinse dishes twice, the final rinse being in hot water.

Dishwashing detergent must be alkalies in nature, increase witting actions, dissolve stains, emulsify fats, and protective for the dishes as well as the machines.

Automatic dishwashers represent a tremendous saving in time and effort; they minimize breakage through reduced handling of dishes; they help keep the kitchen neater and more clutter-free; and clean-up after entertaining is simplified. These are benefits that have much appeal to consumers.

Automatic dishwashing is superior to hand dishwashing in other ways. One of the most important of these is the manner in which it sanitizes dishes. A study by the University of Louisville School of medicine pointed out that the average bacteria count for all machine washed dishes in their study was less than 1 per plate, while the bacteria count on dishes washed by hand during the same test averaged 390 per plate. Bearing in mind that bacteria are ubiquitous ever present on our hands-on working surfaces on dish cloths, sponges, dishtowels and the like it is not surprising that some of the hand washed dishes in this study had a bacteria count as high as 16,000. All of the machine washed dishes easily met the public health standard of 100 bacteria or less per plate, a level recognized by health authorities as safe and attained.

Silver Room or Plate Room

It is the room which holds the complete stock of silver required for the service of all meals, together with a slight surplus stock.

Storage

(i) Large silver, such as flats, salvers, Soup Tureens, Cloches etc. are stored in shelves.

(ii) All shelves should be labeled showing where each different item goes.

(iii) The heavier items should go on the lower side and the smaller and lighter items on the shelved higher up.

(iv) All cutlery and flat ware, together with the smaller items of silvers such as ash trays, cruets, butter dishes, special equipment, table numbers, menu holders etc. are best stored in drawers lined with green baize. This helps to prevent noise and stops cutlery sliding about the drawer when it is opened and closed and so becoming scratched and marked.

Silver Cleaning Methods

The cleanliness of all service is most important. These are various methods of silver cleaning. They are:

1. Burnishing Machine
2. Polivit
3. Plate Powder
4. Sliver Dip

The larger establishment use a burnishing machine whereas the smaller establishment, which possibly could not afford a burnishing machine, would use "silver dip".

1. Burnishing Machine

This is a revolving drum with a safety shield. It may be plumbed into the mains or remain portable with the water being poured in by means of a hose from a tap.

(i) Depending on the size of the burnishing machine in use. It may be plumbed into the mains or remain portable with the water being poured in my beans of a hose from a tap.

(ii) Depending on the size of the burnishing machine in use. It may be divided into compartments to hold specific sizes of silver.

(iii) I may also be possible to extend a rod through the center of the drum from one end to the center of the drum from one end to the other. The rod is removable and is passed through the handles of teapots, coffee pots, milk jugs, sugar basins etc. to hold them in position while the drum is revolving.

(iv) In order for the burnishing machine to run effectively and efficiently it is approximately half-full of ball bearings.

(v) To these, certain amount of soap power is added to the

makers instructions. After the silver is placed inside and clamped down tightly. The main water supply is then turned on to ensure a constant flow of water. If the machine is not plumbed in then water should be poured into the drum until the ball-bearings are covered before the lid is clamped down. The machine is then switched on.

(vi) As the drum revolves the mixture of water and soap powder acts as a lubricant between the silver and the ball bearings. Thus any tarnish is removed but the silver is not scratched.

(vii) On being removed from the burnishing machine the silver should be rinsed in hot water and dried with a clean tea cloth.

(viii) This method if silver cleaning keeps the silver in good condition with minimum effort and given a lasting polish.

(ix) The ball bearings must always be kept covered with the water otherwise they rust very easily.

2. Polivit Method

(i) It is an aluminium metal shed containing holes which is best used in an enamel or galvanized iron bowl.

(ii) The polivit is placed in the board together with some soda.

(iii) The silver to be cleaned is then put into the bowl, ensuring that at least one piece of silver has contact with the polivit sufficient boiling water.

(iv) A Chemical reaction takes place between the polivit, soda, boiling water and silver, which causes the tarnish to be lifted.

(v) After 3 to 4 minutes the sliver should be removed from the bowl and placed into a second bowl of boiling water and rinsed and then the silver is allowed to drain and then polished with a clean, dry tea cloth.

3. Plate Powder

This is a pink powder which needs mixing with a little methylated spirit to obtains smooth paste the reason for using methylated spirit to mix the powder is that when the pastes rubbed on the article the spirit evaporates much more quickly than would water and the silver is therefore ready for polishing move quickly. If, however methylated spirit is not available, then water may be used.

Cleaning Procedure

(i) The smooth paste, once prepared is rubbed onto the article being cleaned with a clean piece of cloth the paste must be rubbed well to remove all tarnish. The article is then left until the paste has dried and the paste is then rubbed off with a clean cloth. It is advisable to rinse the article well in very hot water and to give a final polish with a clean dry tea cloth.

(ii) When silver is cleaned that has a design with engraving on it, a small toothbrush may be used to brush the paste into the design and clean one used to remove it.

Silver Dip

(i) First the silver which has to be cleaned is cleaned in hot water.

(ii) Silver dip is a pink colour liquid, which must be used in a plastic bowl.

(iii) The silver to be cleaned is placed into wire basket and dipped into the plastic bowl containing silver dip.

(iv) All the silver articles being cleaned should be covered by the liquid.

(v) The silver should be left in the bowl only a very short while and then lifted out and drained.

(vi) After draining it is placed in warm water, rinsed and then polished with a clean dry tea cloth.

(vii) It is harder on the silver than the other methods because of the chemical reaction between the liquid and the silver.

(viii) The method is very quick and produces good results.

Other Forms of Silver Cleaning

1. There are many other proprietary brands of silver cleaning material in the market.
2. Even silver can be cleaned in hot water with a little vinegar or lemon juice added to it, in emergency.

Wash up

It's a area where all used crockery and cattery are come from the restaurant through stewards and clean by kitchen porters. This area is very important for service professional in rush hours back-to-back cleaning of crockery and cutlery is very important. And this very major role in food and beverage department. In wash up area now-a-day dish washing machine was ensemble. The process of dish washing is very flow. The following process required for the washing machine in wash-up area.

1. First food is scraped out manual.
2. Second plates are kept in bent position in stand.
3. Third hot water shower.
4. Forth hot water plus detergent.
5. Fifth again hot water.
6. Sixth hot air for dry of thing.
7. Last is clean equipment comes. All this is a computerized process. After clean equipment comes, whipped it and stage in racks.

CHAPTER

4

Best Hygiene Practise Concept

OBJECTIVE OF THIS CHAPTER

- Hygiene Importance and Meaning
- Kitchen Hygiene
- Factor for Hygiene Control and Maintain Standard
- Evaluation of Pest and there Procedure
- Food Borne Disease
- Disturbance of Hygiene Control
- Cleaning and Disinfection
- Soil in Kitchens
- Sources of Food Contamination
- Food Hygiene and its Important
- Food Poisoning and its Caused
- Food Spoilage
- Food Contamination
- Prevent Food Spoilage and Food Contamination
- Pest Control
- Identifying and Controlling Presence of Pests
- Principles of HACCP and Assured Safe Catering

Best Hygiene Practise Concept

1. *Why Hygiene is so Important?*

Hygiene is very essential for self, the environment in while we live and for the place where we work. Poor Hygiene can cause food poisoning and the same can be lead to death. Especially for the food industry. Where the best standard of Hygiene is important, because of the following reasons.

1. Study shows that kitchan are major potential risk factor where hygiene control is necessary to eliminate danger for healthy by contaminated food customer come from all over the world poor hygiene can cost us.

- Civil action
- Customer complaints
- Low guest and staff morale
- Waste of food
- Closing of premises

2. *What is Hygiene?*

Self cleanliness, cleanliness of environment, so that one can lead a healthy disease free life.

3. *What is Kitchen Hygiene?*

Delivery of hygiene reliable food. Prevention of food poisoning.

4. *Who can Maintain the Best Hygiene?*

Hygiene is the collective responsibility of all of us we all have to contribute to make the personal hygiene environmental hygiene and work place hygiene at the desired standard.

5. *Main Factor for the Hygiene Control*

- People
- Cleanliness of place of work
- Elimatepests

6. *What is our Hotel's Contributening to Maintain Hygiene Standard Personal Hygiene*

- Training at all level
- Awareness by posters
- Awareness throught briefings

Cleaning in the Hotel

- Cross functional team to build team work
- Training classes of kitchan stewarding, kitchan and service staff
- Timely maintenance of equipment
- Training of proper utilization of equipment
- Training in other units to see their best practices.
- Regular instruction of kitchan, lockers garbage disposal and other areas
- Rewards for maintaining hygiene
- Hygiene manual
- Checklist of cleaning
- Cleaning schedule

7. *Evaluation of Pest*

- Pest control schedule
- Pest control by professional agency

8. *Evaluation Procedure*

- Hygience inspection by hygiene committee twice a month between 1-15 and 16-31st
- Best maintained area will be awarded the shield for the month

People

- Personal hygiene

We Assure that

- Our hands and skin are washed and wiped
- Nose mouth and ears are clean
- Nails are trimed
- Cuts, woundes are properly covered
- Do not smoke in "No smoking" area
- Uniform, clothes are cleane
- Report Illness to hotel doctor positive behaviour in the kitchan and all over hoteal premises

Knowledge of

- Critical raw material/products
- Critical equiment/work surfaces
- Storage temperatures
- Cleaning disinfection methods
- Motivation/discipline

The Most Common Food Born Diseases Are

- Botulinum–Headache, intestinal pain, dizziness
- Perfringes–Stomach or intestinal pain, vomiting
- Staphylococcus–Stomach or instestinal pain, vomiting, aurus diarrhea
- Salmonella–Headache, vomiting, fever, stomach or intestinal pain diarrhea

Disturbance of Hygiene Control

- Low awareness of personal hygiene
- Insufficient cleaning method
- Insufficient awareness by government
- Discipline and legal action
  50%–Insufficient known–how
  25%–Insufficient personal hygiene
  10%–Insufficient cleaning and disinfection (Government–institution for food)

Cleaning and Disinfection

Cleaning

Removing of *Visible Soil* of surfaces, equipment and tools.

Disinfection

Destruction of *Invisible Soil*, micro-organisms, which are still presents after cleaning.

Soil in Kitchens

Fat, protein, starch
Lime-scale
Micro-organisms

Ideal Growth Conditions

Humidity
Temperature
Acidity of substrates
Oxygen demand
Nutrient supply

Sources of Food Contamination

1. Bacterial

Raw food

Insects/pests
Refuse/waste
People

2. Physical

Dirt
Air
Water
Clothes
Equipment
Cigarettes

3. Chemical

Pesticides
Insecticides

What is Food Hygiene?

This is quite simple keeping the food we produce display and sell clean and free contamination.

Why is Food Hygiene Important?

- To ensure our customer do not come to any harm from the food we sell
- To ensure a good reputation and increased
- To provide good working conditions, higher staff moral and lower staff turnover
- To comply with the law
- To contribute to higher profits.

What Other Reasons are There?

Micro-Organisms—The Unseen Enemy

Micro-organisms are tiny living things not plants or animals. They are found everywhere, in the air, in the soil and water, in the on us and in the food we eat. Then can only be seen with the aid of a Microsoft.

Examples of micro-organism are:

Bacteria Most bacteria are harmless and some are beneficial such as used for cheese and yoghurt manufacture. The ones that concern us most are those that cause illness, the pathogens, and those that cause spoilage in food.

Moulds Most moulds are harmless and, in the same way as bacteria. Some are beneficial like penicillium. However some can cause illness, but the main cause for concern is spoilage of food products.

Viruses Viruses are small particles much smaller than bacteria that cannot live on their own. Viruses do not live on food. They invade living cell, even harmless bacteria which may be found in food.

Food Poisoning

Food poisoning is an illness caused by eating contaminated food. The main symptoms are:

- Diarrhea
- Sickness
- Abdominal pain
- Fever
- Nausea

In exceptional cases the victim may collapse or die

The groups of people at greater risk from food poisoning are:

- The very young
- The very old
- Pregnant women people who are already ill

Food poisoning may be caused by

- Bacteria or there toxins
- Viruses
- Chemicals
- Metals

The most important cause of food poisoning in this country is bacteria most foods contain bacteria. We get food poisoning when too many pathogenic bacteria are present in our food when it is eaten (normally large number, but in some cases only a few). These bacteria can reach dangerous levels long before they changes the food in any way you cannot see them, small them or taste them.

Those food which will be eaten without further processing cause the greatest risk. They usually require refrigerated storage and are sometimes called high risk foods. These are:

- All cooked meat and poultry
- Cooked meat products and gravy

- Milk, cream and dairy produce
- Cooked eggs and product made from raw eggs example-mayonnaise
- Shellfish and sea foods
- Cooked rice.

The most common food poisoning bacteria are

- Salmonella–mainly from poultry.
- Staphylococcus–carried by two people in every five.
- Clostridium–found on raw foods such as vegetables and meat.
- Campylobacter–found in infected animals and birds and unpasteurized milk.
- Salmonella is one of the bacteria which cause illness themselves. They grow to large numbers in the food which we then eat.
- Staphylococcus is the kind which produces toxins or poisons in the food. We cannot taste, see or smell these poisons and some cannot destroyed by normal cooking.
- Clostridium cause illness and protect themselves against adverse conditions like high temperature or cleaning chemicals, by producing spores. They are difficult to destroy.
- Campylobacter is transferred on the food. If does not need to grow in large numbers in the food to cause us illness. It can cause severe diarrhea and stomach pain. It can be destroyed by normal cooking.

Food poisoning bacteria need the following conditions in order to grow:

Warmth	Temperature between 5 and 63 degree C with optimum growth at 37
Moisture	All living things need moisture to grow
Food	Normally high in protein
Time	One bacteria divides into two every 10-20 minutes given the right conditions.

Food Spoilage

- Food spoilage can be caused by micro-organisms and unlink food poisoning it has noticeable cliects on the food, Spoilage causes the food to discolour, smell or become slimy. These effect are obvious and the food must be offered for consumption or sale.

- Care has to be taken with the handling, storage and shelf life of perishable foods to ensure that spoilage does not start in your premises. In commercial terms this could lead to dissatisfied customers and reduced sales.

How does food become contaminated?

These are two sorts of contamination

1. *Microbiological:* This is when micro-organisms get onto food.
2. *Physical:* This is when foreign substances, example chemicals or foreign matter, example glass, stone, metal, get into the food.

Where do contaminations come from?

- The person
- Raw food
- Equipment and machinery
- Premises
- Refuse and waste food
- Pests
- Dirt and dust

Contamination can occur directly from the source of the food poisoning bacteria to the food or indirectly from raw foods to cooked via a knife cloth or work surface.

This is called CROSS CONTAMINATION.

What can we done to prevent food poisoning and food spoilage?

We do not suffer the symptoms of food poisoning every time we eat high risk food. For food poisoning to occur there has usually been a breakdown in food hygiene practice which has allowed the micro-organism to live and grow.

Once again the conditions bacteria need to grow are:

- Warmth
- Moisture
- Food
- Time
- Some require oxygen and some don't

In normally circumstances we have no control over the moisture content of the chosen food. We can however control the temperature of the food and the time for which we hold it, making sure we:

- Protect the food from contamination
- Prevent any bacteria in the food from multiplying

This can be achieved by

Protection	Prevention
• Good personal hygiene	Correct temperature
• Hygienic practices control	
• Good storage and rotation	Some from of food preservation
• Cleaning	
• Good housekeeping	
• Pest control	

Prevention of Contamination

To prevent the risk of contamination always follow good hygienic practices.

1. Never use or offer for sale food which has passed its shelf life.
2. Never mix cooked any raw foods or use the same utensils on both products.
3. Avoid directly handling fresh foods.
4. Never blow into bags to open them.
5. Never use wrapping materials or food that has been on the floor.
6. Never lick your fingers when handling food or wrapping materials.
7. Wash your hands frequently throughout the day.
8. Always ensure your equipment and utensil are kept clean.
9. Keep damaged stock or goods to be returned separate from other goods.
10. Maintain the highest standards of personal hygiene at all times.

Pest Control

A food pest is one that lives in or on our food. Common food pest include.

- Rodents—Rats and mice
- Insects—Flies, cockroaches, ants
- Birds—Pigeons, sparrows, starlings

These pests need to controlled to:

- Prevent the spread of disease–rodents, flies, cockroaches and birds are all capable of spreading disease.

- Prevent damage–every year thousands of pounds worth of damage is caused to the structure and fabric of building by pests.
- Reduce wastage of food–contamination of food by pests leads to complaints and is the main reason for the destruction of large quantities of food product.
- Comply with the law–the law requires premises to be kept free from pest infestation.

Identifying and Controlling Presence of Pests

1. Cleaning of live and dead bodies, droppings.
2. Watching out for damage marks, spillage unusual smell footprints, rodent smears. Loss of small amounts of food.
3. Electric Fly Killers.
4. Chemical, Physical and Biological agents for pest control may be used BUT under supervision.

Before usage of pesticides, the food, equipment etc. must be covered.

Principles of HACCP and Assured Safe Catering

Firstly hazards have to be identified from the start of the process through to the finish. Every thin must be looked at and followed through. The risk of those hazards have to be assessed and a decision made as to whether the hazard. If not controlled or limited, will get through to customer's. This become a critical point in the process and it needs to be controlled.

The critical control point is monitored in various ways and the preventative measures at that point must be kept within the target and tolerances set. Action must be taken when the preventative measure is not going to prevent the hazard happening.

The HACCP Assured Safe Catering plan needs to be checked from time to time to ensure there is control of food safely.

1. Personnel must were clean special and protective Centiliter so thing Colour Code Change daily not washed in kitchen gloves etc. No working clothes in kitchen.
2. Cuts, bruises must be covered with water proof dressings.
3. Smoking must be prohibited.
4. Hand wash facilities must be adequate and separate from basins for cleaning equipments /utensils.

OVERVIEW OF HACCP/ASSURED SAFE CATERING

Hazard Analysis Critical Control Point

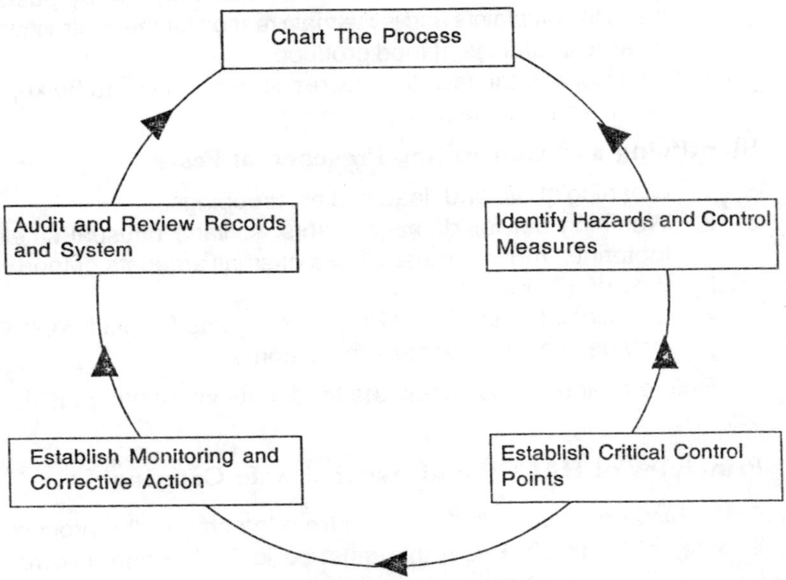

PERSONAL Hygiene

5. Long nails, sneezing, loose hair direct handling of food must be prohibited.
6. Hand must be washed—Starting work after cleaning the food/ refuse sneezing etc.
7. Illness must be reported.
8. Maintenance of locker rooms.
9. Washroom away from food handling areas.
10. Health screening at the time employment or travel.
11. Toilets–
    - Not open directly to food handling areas
    - Ventilation
    - Non–hand operated taps and soap
    - Dispensers.
12. Hygiene training.

Personal Hygiene

Food handlers are the most frequent source of contamination of food. You have a moral and legal responsibility to observe high standards of personal hygiene and you must do everything you can to ensure your actions do not result in the contamination of the products and sell.

Hands and Skin

Hands are in contact with food all the time and they are the main method of transferring contamination.

Wash your hand thoroughly and frequently throughout the day using hot water, unscented soap, a nail brush and clean towel. Was hand basins with three times must be provided in all food premises.

Always wash your hands—

- After using the WC–all WCs for use by food handlers must display a notice stating "now wash your hand."
- Before starting your work and when returning to work after a break during your working day.
- After eating, smoking or blowing your nose.
- After handling waste food and refuse.
- Between handling raw food and cooked foods.
- After carrying out any cleaning activity.

Finger nails should be very short and clean with no nail varnish.

Jewellery and Perfume

Take off watches, brooches, jeweled rings or earrings as they can harbor dirt and bacteria and could drop into food.

Avoid strong smelling perfumes as these can taint food product.

The Hair

The average human head sheds about 50 hair each day, and these along with bacteria from the scale may contaminate food products.

- You must were clean head coverings which completely enclose the hair.
- You should never comb your hair whilst wearing protective clothing as hair may end up on your shoulders and then in the food.

Smoking

It is against the law for food handlers to smoke while working in food rooms. You should only smoke in a designated area. This is because you touch your lips with your hands when smoking and may transfer bacteria to food. Also

- Smoking encourages coughing
- Ash and cigarette ends may find their way into food product.

Protective Clothing

All food handlers should ware clean and washable protective clothes. This protective clothing is designed to protect the food from you and should therefore be worn correctly and only while at work.

Do not keep outdoor clothes in food rooms. Store protective clothing properly. Keep hats and coat away from food or packaging. Foot ware should have low heels, be enclosed, have non-slip soles and be kept clean.

Cuts and Sports

These provide an ideal place for bacteria to multiply. They should be covered with a brightly coloured (normally blue), clean, waterproof dressing. Remember, even a clean cut that has almost healed is a breeding ground for bacteria so keep it cover.

Check that the first aid box in your work area is regularly restocked with bright blue waterproof dressings.

Reporting Illness

Anyone suffering from diarrhea vomiting, skin infections heavy colds and discharges from the eyes or ears should not handle food.

If you are ill with this type of illness, you must notify your supervisors and get medical attention. You will not normally be allowed to return to work until medical clearance has been given. This is especially important in the case of food poisoning illness. Some people termed as "carrier" can carry food poisoning bacteria in there system after recovering from the infection or perhaps if they have not suffered any obvious symptoms.

CHAPTER

5

Basic Standards

OBJECTIVE OF THIS CHAPTER

- Hygiene Importance and Meaning
- Cleaning Equipments and Materials
- Washing and Refuse Disposal
- Reducing Risk of Infestation
- Mechanical Action
- Contact Time of Cleaning
- Removal of Tea/Coffee Stains
- Adhering Oil
- Rust Formation/Pitting Corrosion
- Decolouration of the Dishes
- Starch Deposit on Tableware
- Dryness of Dishes after Operation
- Greasy Glassware/Blue Glass
- White Deposit on Glassware
- Speckles on Glassware
- Rules for Effective Warewashing
- Cleanings Disinfection

- Factor in a Dishwash Process
- Machine Overforming
- Manual Dishwash V/s Machine Dishwash

HOW TO CLEAN THE KITCHEN

Cleaning Equipments and Materials

1. Cloths, Mops, Brushes– cleaned and dried after use.
2. Brushes and Mops Head-Washed in hot water, soaked overnight in sanitizer, rinsed and dried quickly.
3. Mop Buckets–dried stored inverted.
4. Maximize use of disposable material.
5. Rewashing and drying outside the kitchen area.

Washing

1. Separate sinks for utensil and hand washing buckets with solutions used for cleaning must not be emptied into the sinks.
2. Scrapping pre-rinsing, soaking procedures etc.
3. Work flow must be unidiloctional.
4. Blocked sinks drains must be guarded against.
5. State of finish to washed items satisfactory?

Refuse Disposal

1. Cleaning and maintenance.
2. Adequate supply of bind, stacking, lids, stands, with lids.
3. Periodicity of emptying.
4. Separate areas for refuse collections, storage and disposal.

Reducing Risk of Infestation

1. Clean premises and refuse areas.
2. Lids on waste bins which are washed after emptying.
3. Covered food.
4. Prompt cleaning of spillages.
5. Clean drains.

Mechanical Action

1. Contributes to 70 per cent of cleaning process.
2. Kinetic energy of liquid jet.

3. Interaction between lower and upper wash arms.
4. Nozzle diameter.
5. Foam generation.
6. Pump capacity.

Contact Time of Cleaning

A minimum compactly of 60 seconds is necessary for efficient cleaning. However, cycle times of up to 120 seconds are also possible depending upon the capacity of the machine.

The cycle time of 120 seconds cannot be reduced to 80 second by higher dosages of the liquids for two reasons:

1. As the alkalinity conditions to remove certain kinds of soil are not met, and
2. The foaming in the machine increases.

Removal of Tea/Coffee Stains

Tea and coffee stains may be removed by soaking in water for 10 minutes. Bleach must not be used on silver cutlery as it blackens cutlery.

Detergents with strong polyphosphates can effectively remove these stains. (Additionally, they can finely distribute leftovers in the cleaning solution thus avoiding new dirt accumulation to a large extent).

However, tea and coffee stains remain after washing due to the following reasons:

1. Inadequate concentration of detergent or wash temperature
2. High water hardness and
3. Insufficient pump pressure
4. Long lead time between adherence of stains and the washing of the glassware.

Adhering Oil

Adhering oil is generally caused due to:

1. Insufficient mechanical washing due to a damaged pump, Centiliter sagged pump filters, Centiliter sagged sprayers, leaking washing arms. Level of washing water or foam or too low a cavitations of the pump or
2. Rinsing shadows.

Rust Formation/Pitting Corrosion

The cause of the rust formation are inferior metal insufficient final rising, too low a dosage (pH), or the water containing too much chloride (>150ppm Maximum).

Decolouration of the Dishes

Excessive presence of heavy metals (iron and manganese) cause discolorations and varnish-like coating on the machine as well as the utensil. Traces of copper also produce the above effect.

Starch Deposit on Tableware

In the case of starch deposit on the tableware, the following have been observed be the usual causes:

1. Insufficient dosage of detergent.
2. Per-rinsing temperature too high.
3. Insufficient mechanical washing.
4. Too much bath soiling.
5. Too high a temperature of lowerators.
6. Use of certain instant binding agent.

Are the Dishes Completely Dry after Rinsins Operation?

The dishes are not completely dry after the rinsing operation as steam is present in the tank which condenses on the dishes. The above problem can be solved by having a longer conveyor belt.

However, the drying of the dishes can be improved by adjusting of the rinse- aid, by appropriate usage of the racks and baskets, by removing the rinsing shadows, by cleaning the suction fan and by temperature drying of the air.

Temperature

Soil removal
Melting fats
Denaturation of proteins swelling of starches
Drying
Sanitizing.

Temperature

The following temperatures must be maintained for the different stages of MWW:

Pre-rinse (45-55°C)
Main wash using detergent

Wash tank 1 55-60°C
Wash tank 2 60-65°C
Pressure rinse (65-75°C)
Final rinse (80-85°C)

- Proteins
- Thermal shock

Scale Build-up

- Increased water hardness
- Detergent concentration too low
- Variable water hardness
- Water softener not working properly
- Wash temperature too high.

Greasy Glassware/Blue Glass

Glassware becomes greasy due to inappropriate.

Dosage (Overdosing) of the rinse-aid and inappropriate amount and temperature of final rinse water.

White Deposit on Glassware

The white deposit on the glassware may be line deposit due to the hardness of water. In that event, water treatment is advisable. Pre-soaking the lime deposit in an acidic product will help.

It may also be due to the final rinsing pattern in which case the sprayers must be cleaned, and the water pressure corrected.

The right basket must also be used. It must also be checked if the curtain are preventing the final rinsing.

Speckles on Glassware

The appearance of speckles on glassware depends upon:

1. The type of soiling
2. Soiling of machine especially under rime and
3. Racks, especially on possibility of rinsing
4. Cleanliness of the water being used.

Ten Operating Rules for Effective Warewashing

- Remove as many scrape as possible
- Sort cutlery/crockery by size/type
- Turn glasses and cup upside down
- Mix cutlery handles downwards

- Use the right baskets
- Pre-soak heavily soiled dishes
- Use a spray jet
- Feed baskets in the right direction
- Wash glasses separately
- Remove clean cutlery and crockery.

Cleaning as Disinfection

Cleaning	*Disinfection*
Floor	Cutting boards
Walls	Working surfaces
Drains	Slicing
Machines	Equipment legs
Utensils Handles on	Drawers, doors

Factor in a Dishwash Process

The main factors in a dishwash process are:

1. Temperature
2. Contact time
3. Mechanical action
4. Water quality
5. Detergent
6. Soil
7. Type of dishes
8. Stacking of the dishes

Machine Over Forming

1. Excessive soiling in wash time
2. Excessive detergent concentration
3. Insufficient rinse-aid
4. Wash tank temperature too low (<55°C)
5. Rinse economizer incorrectly adjusted
6. Drain overflow partially obstructed
7. Detergent on rinse-aid contaminated

PROBLEM DIAGNOSIS

Excessive Detergent Consumption

1. Detergent concentration too high
2. Leaking drain valve

3. Leaking fill valve
4. Excessive Filling (Manual Fill)
5. Excessive dilution due to continuous rising
6. Excessive dilution due to high rinse water pressure
7. Rinse economizer (where filled) not adjusted correctly
8. Sumatic doser switched on before wash tank is full
9. Detergent probe scaled up
10. Soiling of electrodes.

Manual Dishwash V/s. Machine Dishwash

Manual Dishwashing		*Machine Dishwashing*
	MECHANICAL	
Relatively high pressure depended on operator and soil type		Limited pressure by wash jets articles are free standing
	CHEMICAL	
Skin contact limits use of strong chemicals		Strong and aggressive chemicals, high concentrations
	THERMAL	
Temperature max 50°C		High temp up to 3/90°C possible
	TIME	
Labour intensive and chow		Very high throughput

Advantages of Machine Dishwashing

- Good result
- Low total cost
- High speed
- Hygienic.

CHAPTER

6

Standard Operation Procedure

OBJECTIVE OF THIS CHAPTER

- Standard Operation Procedure
- Check List for Cleaning Kitchen Equipments and Areas
- Check List for Personal Hygiene and General Cleanliness
- Formats
- Inventory Control and Management
- Working Capital Management
- Example of Kitchen Stewarding Formats

SOP No. 1: SOP OF PEST CONTROL

Objective: To keep entire kitchen area pest and rodent free.

Scope: It shall include receiving, kitchen, storage and butchery.

Responsibility: Line staff kitchen and kitchen stewarding, shift supervisor, executive house keeper, executive chef and kitchen stewarding manager.

Procedure:

1. Holes, drains and other places where pest are likely to gain entry should be kept closed/sealed.
2. All windows, exhaust fan opening should be covered with sieve/mesh to prevent entry of flying insects.
3. The entire raw material/final product should be stacked away from wall.
4. Use flycatchers at appropriate locations in premises.
5. Put rat traps (Rodabox) where their rats are likely enters in to kitchen premises.
6. Waste matter/garbage should not be allowed to keep inside the kitchen and if necessary it shall be covered with tight cover.
7. Reputed pesticide agency should be appointed for pest control work in factory premises and all pest control activity should be monitored by house keeping department.
8. In house pest management could be there.
9. Appropriate pesticide/insecticide shall be permitted only under precaution and restrictions that will protect against contamination of food, food contact surface and serving material.

Approved by: ____________ Issued by: ____________ Issue No. 01

Date: __________ Designation: __________ Checked by: __________

Date: ____________ Revision No. ____________

SOP No. 2: SOP OF CROSS CONTAMINATION

Objective: To prevent cross contamination and spreading of food spoilage/pathogenic micro-organisms while doing various activities in the kitchen.

Scope: Whole kitchen, storage and receiving area shall be covered in this SOP.

Responsibility: Line staff kitchen, kitchen stewarding, house keeping, stores and receiving executive chef, executive house keeper and kitchen stewarding manager.

Procedure:

1. Cleaning out of place is carried out after the regular interval and when operation is stopped and there is no product left.
2. Ensure everyday that equipment doesn't contain any deposit in it which may lead to contamination of the food.
3. Clean and sanitize each equipment/machine/crockery as per the proper cleaning schedule.
4. Good Hygienic Practices should be followed by all staff whosoever comes in contact directly or indirectly with raw and finished goods.
5. Use appropriate pesticide/insecticide and disinfectants on identified all points through which there is a chance of entry of rodents and pests in the factory.
6. Equipments, if possible may be dismantled wherever possible for well and complete cleaning.
7. Prevent any leakage of oil grease from the equipment that may be contaminating food product.
8. All the machines, utensils and equipments that are come directly or indirectly in to contact of food should be sanitized before processing starts.

Food grade and non-food grade material should be kept separately to prevent cross contamination.

Approved by: _____________ Issued by: _____________ Issue No. 01

Date: ___________ Designation: ___________ Checked by: ___________

Date: _____________ Revision No. _____________

SOP No. 3: SOP OF GOOD HYGIENIC PRACTICES (PERSONNEL HYGIENE)

Objective: Maintaining an appropriate degree of personal cleaning to ensure that the person comes directly/indirectly in to the contact with food is not likely to contaminate food.

Scope: Good hygienic practices cover receiving, storage, kitchen, packaging area of the hotel.

Procedure:

1. Maintaining an appropriate degree of personnel cleanliness.
2. Behaving and operating in an appropriate manner.
3. It is mandatory for all the persons before entering into kitchen area to wash and sanitize their hands with soap and approved sanitizer.
4. Apron without pockets and buttons are provided to the cooks. All unsecured jewelry and other objects that might fall into food, equipment or container are removed before entrance to the kitchen section.
5. Hand sanitization is mandatory at the interval of one hour during shift in the case of raw meat handling.
6. Kitchen workforce is regularly checked for adequate personal cleanliness for hair cut, nails, cuts or wounds, free from any contagious disease.
7. It is mandatory for all to be wearing hairnets, headbands, caps or other effective hair restraints before entering the kitchen section/processing section.
8. Any worker who leaves the kitchen vicinity should deposit his hairnets and Apron to the shift supervisor. Once the cook performs all the sanitization activities for personal hygiene and then only the supervisor should allow and return the kitchen dress.
9. Eating food, drinking beverages, chewing gum/tobacco/gutkha is strictly prohibited inside the plant.
10. All the visitors to food manufacturing, processing or handling area must wear protective clothing and adhere to other personal hygiene provisions (PHP).

11. Any person who by medical examination or supervisory observation, is shown to have or appears to have, an illness, open lesion, including boils, sores, or infected wounds, or any other abnormal source of microbicidal contamination by which there is a reasonable possibility of food, food contact surfaces, or food serving materials becoming contaminated, is excluded from any operations until the condition is corrected.

Approved by: ____________Issued by:_____________Issue No. 01

Date: __________Designation: __________Checked by:__________

Date: ____________ Revision No. ____________

SOP No. 4: SOP OF TRAINING

Objective: To make employees trained, who will understand the process much easily and facilitate maximum production and minimum rejection.

Scope: It shall covers entire workforce of the unit.

Responsibility: supervisors, kitchen stewarding manager and training manager.

Procedure:

1. Competence required is evaluated for all levels.
2. The available staff is verified against the required competence.
3. Shortfalls in the competence required are identified.
4. Training is provided on the shortfalls.
5. Effectiveness of the training provided is evaluated on the job and personal interview within 8-10 days.
6. The general topics of training are as follows:
   - 6.1. Personal Hygiene.
   - 6.2. Food safety.
   - 6.3. Cleaning of all electrical kitchen equipments.
   - 6.4. Garbage segregation and disposal.
   - 6.5. Cleaning of dish washer.
   - 6.6. Cleaning of wall and other washable surfaces.
   - 6.7. Cleaning and Sabitizing of Chopping Boards.

Approved by: ______________ Issued by:________ Issue No. 01

Date: __________ Designation: __________ Checked by:__________

Date: ____________ Revision No. ____________

SOP No. 5: AREA: FLOOR /WALL AND OTHER WASHABLE SURFACES LIKE STAIRS/RAILINGS

Objective: To keep area clean and free from bacterial growth.

Frequency: In every shift, weekly, monthly.

Scope: Whole kitchen, service back area and stairs shall be covered in this sop.

Supplies Required: Broom, bucket, cloth, scrubber, dustpan, and water.

Responsibility: Line staff, shift supervisor and kitchen stewarding manager.

Procedure:

1. Sweep and remove all the trash from the floor with push broom.
2. In a clean bucket mix detergent in 1ltr hot water.
3. Put the detergent on the surface/floor.
4. Scrub the floor with brush.
5. Squeeze the water from the floor.
6. Squeeze the mop to remove excess water and thoroughly mop the floor 2-3 times.
7. Mop again with clean cloth till dry.
8. Follow the similar procedure at the fixed intervals.

Monthly Cleaning Steps

1. Remove all the shelves and movable equipments/machinery from the respective locations.
2. Clean the floor by applying steps 1 to 5 as mentioned in the weekly cleaning steps.
3. Place all the shelves and equipments back to their original location.

1.2. AREA: CEILINGS, FANS AND LIGHT FIXTURES

Frequency: Monthly

Supplies Required: Broom, dust cloth, cob web removers.

Cleaning Steps

1. Cleaning can be done along with the walls and windows.
2. Use a ladder or stool to climb.

3. Clean the ceiling with a wet cloth/duster
4. Wipe the fans with a dry cloth followed by a wet cloth.
5. Remove the cob webs with a broom.
6. Clean the light fixtures with a dry cloth.

Approved by:______________Issued by:______________Issue No. 01

Date:___________Designation: __________Checked by:___________

Date: ______________ Revision No. _____________

SOP No. 6: AREA: FOOD CONTACT SURFACES

Objective: To keep work counter clean and prevent to cross contamination.

Frequency: After each use.

Scope: It shall include all kitchen and service work counters.

Supplies Required: Clean cloth, paper towels, hot water (70-80 degree C).

Chemical Required: D2.2 suma extra/D2.3l suma multi (Johnson Diversey).

Sanitizer Required: D-10 suma bac (Johnson Diversey).

Responsibility:

Procedure:

Line staff, shift supervisor and kitchen stewarding manager.

1. Sweep off all the left over material from the surface with a clean dry cloth.
2. Make a solution of suma extra/suma multi in hot water (70-80 deg C) (for normal soiling 20ml in 1ltr, for heavy soiling 50ml in 1ltr.)
3. Clean the surface thoroughly using this solution.
4. Dilute D-10 sumabac solution at the rate of 20ml in 1ltr water.
5. Use this solution to wipe all surface with a clean cloth or spray the diluted sanitizer on to the table top surface evenly.
6. Wipe it with paper towel.
7. DO NOT use water on these areas after the application of this sanitizer solution.

Approved by:____________ Issued by:____________ Issue No. 01

Date:__________ Designation:__________ Checked by:__________

Date:____________ Revision No. ____________

SOP No. 7: AREA : POT WASH AND EQUIPMENT ATTACHMENTS

Objective: To keep pot wash area clean and tidy to prevent cross contamination.

Scope: All pot wash areas covered in this SOP.

Frequency: After each use.

Supplies Required: Scrubber, hot water.

Chemical Required: D1.2Y suma det /D2.2 suma extra/suma multi. (Johnson Diversey).

Responsibility:

Procedure:

1. Sinks and work surfaces should be cleaned before each use.
2. Scrape off the extra left over material with the scrubber.
3. Dip the greasy utensils in the hot water for 2-3 min.
4. Items to be cleaned should be washed first in a clean detergent solution at approximately 50 deg Cusing brush or dish mop.
5. Rinse with water (50-60 deg C) thoroughly to remove all traces of detergent and residual material.
6. Clean utensils and equipments should be stored in a clean area more than 20cm off the floor for protection from splash, dust and contact with food.

Approved by: ____________Issued by:__________Issue No. 01

Date: __________Designation: __________Checked by:__________

Date: ____________ Revision No. __________

SOP No. 8: AREA: STORAGE AREA

Objective: To keep area clean and free from bacterial growth.

Scope: All kitchen and service areas shall be covered in this SOP.

Frequency: Daily/weekly.

Supplies Required: Broom, dust pan, vacuum cleaner, mop, bucket, water.

Sanitizer Required: D10 suma bac (Johnson Diversey).

Chemical Required: D2.2 suma extra/D2.3l 15ml in 1 ltr water (Johnson Diversey).

Responsibility: Line staff, shift supervisor and kitchen stewarding manager.

Procedure:

1. Using dry clean cloth dust off the racks/shelves in the storage area.
2. Dust off any dirt on the ingredients boxes/containers on the shelf and remove any spilled material.
3. Clean the floor in the storage area as mentioned in the daily cleaning steps of the floor.

Weekly Cleaning Steps

1. Remove ingredients from the shelves. Place the ingredients either on other shelf, table or pallet. DO NOT put any ingredients on the floor.
2. Using dry clean cloth dust off the racks/shelves in the storage area.
3. Dust off the ingredient boxes/containers and put them back on the shelf. Take care to put any liquid ingredient on the bottom shelf.
4. Clean the floor in the storage area as mentioned in the weekly cleaning steps for the floor.

Approved by: ______________ Issued by: ______________ Issue No. 01

Date: ___________ Designation: ___________ Checked by: ___________

Date: ______________ Revision No. ______________

SOP No. 9: AREA: BAKING OVEN

Objective: To prevent bacterial growth.
Scope: Bakery oven covered in this SOP.
Frequency: Monthly.
Supplies Required: Clean cloth, water, scrubber.
Chemical Required: D9–suma grill oven cleanser (Johnson Diversey).
Responsibility: Line staff, shift supervisor and kitchen stewarding manager.

Procedure:

1. Wipe off any dry material inside the oven with the clean cloth.
2. Pre heat the oven at > 200°C.
3. Spray D9 solution on the inside of the oven over the dirty area. Allow it to stay for 5 min to 10 min.
4. Take a clean wet cloth and scrap off all the material.

1.9 Clean insect killer tray: The insect killer tray should be removed daily. Empty the insect tray, wash with water, sanitize with a diluted solution of D10 suma bac, dry and place back under the trapper.

1.10 Clean AC filters: The AC filters should be removed from the AC once in a month. The filter is taken out, dirt is removed with the brush. Wash with water. Dry and place it back into the AC.

1.11 Clean garbage bins: Should be cleaned daily. Remove the plastic bag and dispose off the garbage. Clean the bins thoroughly with water and detergent.

1.12 Clean weighing machines and outer machine surfaces: All the machines should be cleaned daily and whenever dirty in between the production. Wipe off the dust with clean cloth. Scrub the surface if required with the scrubber/brush. Apply few drops of teepol solution on to the surface and then wipe it dry with the clean cloth.

Approved by: ____________ Issued by: ____________ Issue No. 01

Date: __________ Designation: __________ Checked by: __________

Date: ____________ Revision No. ____________

SOP No. 10: DOUGH DIVIDER /MIXER CLEANING AND CHOCOLATE MELTING MACHINE

Objective: To keep the equipment clean and free from bacterial growth.
Scope: This SOP covered bakery equipment.
Frequency: Daily/weekly.
Supplies Required: Duster, bucket, dry cloth.
Chemical Required: D2.2 suma extra. (Johnson Diversey).
Responsibility: Line staff, shift supervisor and kitchen stewarding manager.

Procedure:

1. Scrub off the inside surface with clean cloth.
2. Make a mixer of D2.2 suma extra with hot water 20ml in 1 ltr in a bucket.
3. Clean the inside of the machine thoroughly with the D2.2 suma extra solution.
4. Rinse with water.
5. Wipe it dry with the clean cloth.

Weekly Cleaning Steps

1. Dismantle all the parts of the machine.
2. Clean with D2.2 suma extra solution.
3. Rinse thoroughly with water.
4. Wipe it dry with a clean cloth.

1.13 CHOCOLATE MELTING MACHINE

Frequency: Daily

Cleaning Steps

1. Preliminary rinse with hot detergent solution.
2. Put the chocolate bowl into the machine.
3. Scrub the extra material.
4. Drain out the water through the nozzle.

Approved by: ______________ Issued by: ______________ Issue No. 01

Date: ___________ Designation: ___________ Checked by: ___________

Date: ______________ Revision No. ______________

SOP No. 11. CLEANING OF POTATO PEELER

Objective: To reduce bacterial growth.
Frequency: After every use.
Supplies Required: Bucket, hand brush.
Chemical Required: D2.2 suma extra/D2.3l suma multi (Johnson Diversey).
Responsibility: Line staff, shift supervisor and kitchen stewarding manager.

Procedure:

Interior Cleaning

1. Un plug the machine from electrical socket/panels.
2. Open up the potato peeler cover.
3. Take out potato pulp from inner surface with help of hand brush with hard bristles.
4. Then apply soap solution mixture on the inner surface scrub with hand brush.
5. Rinse well with water.

Exterior Cleaning

1. Un plug the machine from electrical socket/panels.
2. Scrub the outer surfaces with abrasive pad and soap solution mixture.
3. Wipe the outer surfaces with damp cloth or duster.
4. Do not rinse the outer surfaces with water, it may cause to electrical hazards.
5. Pay special attention to the drainage pipe; it will go choked very frequently, If found choked, clean the drainage pipe.

Approved by: ____________Issued by:____________Issue No. 01

Date: __________Designation: __________Checked by:________

Date: ____________ Revision No. ____________

SOP No. 12: MASALA GRINDER CLEANING

Objective: To keep the equipment clean and free from bacterial growth.

Frequency: Daily/After every shift

Supplies Required: Bucket, duster, scotch brite and water.

Chemical Required: D 2.2 suma extra,/D2.3I suma multi. (Johnson Diversey).

Responsibility: Line staff, shift supervisor and kitchen stewarding manager.

Procedure:

Interior

1. Un plug the machine from electrical socket.
2. Remove the grinding stone from grinder and keep at safe place.
3. Remove the dirties from grinder.
4. Spray luck warm water on the inner surface of grinder to loosened the dirties.
5. Make mixer of suma extra/suma multi with hot water in a bucket.
6. Spray soap solution mixture on inner surfaçe and scrub with scrubber.
7. Ensure no dirty is left in grinder.
8. Rinse well with water.
9. Remove the dirty water from grinder and wipe with damp cloth or duster.
10. Wash the grinding stone with soap solution and scrubber.
11. Wipe the grinding stone and place it in the grinder nicely at there proper angle.
12. Pay special attention to the grinding stone belt, it should clean and well maintained.

Exterior

1. Un plug the machine from electrical socket.
2. Make a soap solution mixture.
3. Apply soap solution mixture on outer surface of grinder with the help of scrubber/sponge and scrub the outer surfaces nicely.
4. Ensure no dirty mark is left.
5. Wipe with clean duster.
6. Wet masala grinder is ready for next use.

Special Note: Do not splash water to rinse the machine it may cause to electrical hazards.

Approved by: ____________ Issued by: ____________ Issue No. 01

Date: ____________ Designation: ____________ Checked by: ____________

Date: ____________ Revision No. ____________

SOP No. 13: CLEANING OF TILTING PAN

Objective: To keep the equipment clean and free from bacterial growth.

Frequency: After every use.

Supplies Required: Spray bottle, scotch brite, duster and water.

Chemical Required: D2.2 suma extra,/D2.3l suma multi. (Johnson Diversey).

Responsibility: Line staff, shift supervisor and kitchen stewarding manager.

Procedure:

Interior

1. When the unit is cool enough to handle, take all removable parts such as drip pans, racks, etc. the pot sink for soaking, scrubbing and rinsing.
2. Spray interior surfaces with. D2.2 suma extra,/ D2.3l suma multi.
3. Allow 5 minutes for solution to soak into and soften soil. On heavily soiled areas or where grease has been baked, agitate soil with a stiff brush.
4. Use damp cloth to pick up the dissolved and loosened grease.
5. Rinse with clean water. Let air dry and reassemble.

Exterior

1. Spray the outside of unit D2.2 suma extra,/D2.3l suma multi. solution. Remove the loosened soil with a damp cloth.
2. Rinse with low pressure clear water and wipe dry with a clean, dry cloth.
3. In case of electrical Steam Kettles ensure that the water does not come in contact with electrical connections.

Important Note: Be sure the entire exterior and areas underneath and behind the equipment are cleaned.

Approved by: ____________ Issued by: ____________ Issue No. 01

Date: __________ Designation: __________ Checked by: __________

Date: ____________ Revision No. ____________

SOP No. 14 : CLEANING OF STAKE OVENS

Objective: To keep the equipment clean and free from bacterial growth.

Frequency: After every shift, weekly, monthly.

Supplies Required: Spray bottle, sponge, hand brush, scotch brite, duster and water.

Chemical Required: D9 suma grill, D2.2 suma extra,/D2.3l suma multi. (Johnson Diversey).

Responsibility: Line staff, shift supervisor and kitchen stewarding manager.

Procedure:

Interior

Spray cleaning procedure.

1. Preheat oven to 150 degree F–turn heat off.
2. While oven surfaces are still warm, wipe the interior with a sponge using D9 suma grill solution.
3. Carbonized food or baked grease may have to be loosened with a stiff brush or scrubber.
4. Use a damp cloth to pick up the dissolved and loosened soil.
5. Wipe with a clean damp cloth.

Metal floor inserters should be removed when they become stained, and cleaned by following method.

* Using any container except aluminium, that will immerse half or more of the inserts, soak the insert in a light foam liquid soap solution in 180° F until the stains can be brushed away. Rinse in Clear water. De-stain the other half. Rinse and replace in the oven after drying.

Note: Be sure the entire exterior and area underneath and behind the ovens are cleaned.

Exterior

Spray degreasing procedure:

1. Spray soiled surfaces with light foaming liquid soap solution using a plastic spray bottle.
2. On heavily soiled areas or where grease has been baked on, agitate soil with a stiff brush.
3. Wipe with a clean damp cloth.

Approved by: ____________ Issued by: ____________ Issue No. 01

Date: __________ Designation: __________ Checked by: __________

Date: ____________ Revision No. ____________

SOP No. 15: CLEANING OF BAKE OVENS

Objective: To avoid any fire hazard and cross contamination.

Frequency: After every shift, weekly, monthly.

Supplies Required: Spray bottle, sponge, hand brush, scotch brite, duster and water.

Chemical Required: D9 suma grill, D2.2 suma extra,/D2.3l suma multi (Johnson Diversey).

Responsibility: Line staff, shift supervisor and kitchen stewarding manager.

Procedure:

Spray Cleaning Procedure

* *Interior*

1. Preheat oven to 150°F–turn off heat.
2. While oven surfaces are still warm, wipe the interior with a sponge using D9 suma grill solution.
3. Baked on grease or carbonized food soil may have to be loosened with a stiff brush or scrubber.
4. Use a damp cloth to pick up the dissolved and loosened soil.
5. Wipe with a clean damp cloth.

* *Exterior*

1. Spray the outside of the oven with light foaming soap solution.
2. Use a damp cloth to pick up the dissolved and loosened soil.
3. Rinse with clear water.
4. Wipe dry with a clean, dry cloth.
5. Keep the sides, front and back of the oven clean at all times.

Approved by: ____________ Issued by: ____________ Issue No. 01

Date: __________ Designation: __________ Checked by: __________

Date: ____________ Revision No. ____________

SOP No. 16: CLEANING OF GRILLS AND GRIDDLES

Objective: To avoid any fire hazard and cross contamination.

Frequency: After every shift.

Supplies Required: Kitting scraper, kitting brush, duster.

Chemical Required: Kitting powder.

Responsibility: Line staff, shift supervisor and kitchen stewarding manager.

Procedure:

1. Scrape all loose soil from the surfaces with kitting scraper as soon as equipment is cool enough to work with.
2. While the surface is still warm apply kitting powder. Allow it to penetrate the soil. Clean the edges and sides of the griddle.
3. Scrape off the loosened soil with kitting brush and wipe with a wet/damp cloth.
4. Empty and wash the scrapings pan and replace it.
5. As griddle start to heat again, brush with food grade vegetable oil. Keep the base of the griddle, the top and sides of the stand, the back plate and the spatter shield thoroughly clean at all times.
6. It is recommended, cleaning of griddles be done after the end of each use period.

Approved by: ____________ Issued by: ____________ Issue No. 01

Date: __________ Designation: __________ Checked by: __________

Date: ____________ Revision No. ____________

SOP No. 17: CLEANING OF DEEP-FRYER

Objective: To stop bacterial growth, cross contamination and fire hazard.

Frequency: Daily in the night shift.

Scope: It shall include banquets kitchen, restaurant kitchen.

Supplies Required: Hand brush, scotch brite.

Chemical Required: D9 suma grill (Johnson Diversey).

Responsibility: Line staff, shift supervisor and kitchen stewarding manager.

Procedure:

1. Allow machine to cool and pump out the oil, remove the filter and transfer the oil to a pre cleaned reservoir.
2. Water mixed with D9 suma grill solution into the deep well. Thoroughly mix the concentrate solution and heat the fryer to 180-200°F. Allow coil to soak solution until completely cleaned. (100ml D9 in 1ltr water).
3. Change the solution with hot water and reheat the fryer to boiling.
4. Brush wash any heavy deposits using the cleaning solution. Brush wash outside surfaces using this same solution.
5. When the tank is completely cleaned, turn the heat off and drain the unit. Add cold water to the solution as it cooling too rapidly. This avoids warping of the metal. Rinse thoroughly with hot water.

Approved by:____________ Issued by:____________ Issue No. 01

Date:__________ Designation:__________ Checked by:__________

Date:____________ Revision No.____________

SOP No. 18: CLEANING OF TABLES-BAIN MARIE

Objective: To stop bacterial growth and cross contamination.

Frequency: Daily in the night shift.

Supplies Required: Hand brush, scotch brite.

Chemical Required: D5.2 suma scale (Johnson Diversey).

Responsibility: Line staff, shift supervisor and kitchen stewarding manager.

Procedure:

Daily

1. Removed food containers to refrigerated storage as soon as serving is completed.
2. Turn off connection and drain water before cleaning.
3. Brush wash all surfaces with a hot solution of D5.2 suma scale solution. (100 ml D5.2 in 1 ltr water)
4. This includes top, back board, front and sides, if baked on foods are stubborn, use a dull metal scraper to remove them.
5. Rinse with hot water.

Periodic Deleing

1. Fill bain marie wells with water and add suma scale of 33 per cent strength.
2. Turn electric connection on and allow hot solution to remain until all lime scale has been removed.
3. Heavy lime scale might require light brushing.

Approved by:_____________Issued by:_____________Issue No. 01

Date:___________Designation:___________Checked by:___________

Date:_____________ Revision No._____________

SOP No. 19: CLEANING OF TOASTERS
(Conveyor Type Toaster)

Objective: To stop bacterial growth and cross contamination.

Frequency: Daily in the night shift.

Supplies Required: Dry cloth/duster.

Chemical Required: D2.2 suma extra/D2.3l suma multi (Johnson Diversey).

Responsibility: Line staff, shift supervisor and kitchen stewarding manager.

Procedure:

1. Un plug toaster. Make certain that during the cleaning operation the electrical parts are not wetted, as this could cause damage to the toaster or serious injury to personnel when toaster is again plugged in.
2. Gently bump toaster on counter to knock all crumbs into crumb tray.
3. Remove crumb tray and wipe clean with D2.2 suma extra/ D2.3l suma multi solution.
4. Rinse in clear water and dry with a clean cloth or duster. *Note:* Do not attempt to clean the heating elements in any manner whatsoever.
5. Move toaster and wipe clean counter surface underneath.
6. Polish with a clean dry cloth.
7. Replace dry clean tray.

Approved by: ____________ Issued by: ____________ Issue No. 01

Date: __________ Designation: __________ Checked by: __________

Date: ____________ Revision No. ____________

SOP No. 20: CLEANING OF FOOD CHOPERS

Objective: To prevent cross contamination.
Frequency: After every use.
Supplies Required: Dry cloth.
Chemical Required: D2.3l sumac, D10 sumac bac (Johnson Diversey).
Responsibility: Line staff, shift supervisor and kitchen stewarding manager.

Procedure:

Dismantle and clean at the end of each use period as follows:

Caution

Disconnect the electrical power and clean the blades with great care, to avoid accidents and injuries. Leave the guard in place until the rest of the machine is cleaned, then remove guard only long enough to clean it and the blade. Use a brush with a long handle.

1. Disassembled parts should be taken to pot sink and flushed with tap water to remove loose soil.
2. Wash these parts in a hot D2.3l suma multi solution.10ml in 1ltr water.
3. Rinse thoroughly with clear water and dip all parts for a sanitizing in D10 sumac bac sanitizing solution.
4. Wipe clean all stationery components using the soap solution. Dry with a clean cloth.

Approved by: ____________ Issued by: ____________ Issue No. 01

Date: __________ Designation: __________ Checked by: __________

Date: ____________ Revision No. ____________

SOP No. 21: CLEANING OF BLENDER

Objective:	To stop bacterial growth and cross contamination.
Frequency:	After every use.
Supplies Required:	Sponge, dry cloth, bucket, water.
Chemical Required:	D2.3l sumac multi, D10 suma bac (Johnson Diversey)
Responsibility:	Line staff, shift supervisor and kitchen stewarding manager.

Procedure:

1. At the end of each use period disconnect the electrical power.
2. Remove the cup, lid and blade assembly to the pot and pan sink. Wash in a detergent.
3. I suma multi solution. Exercise care in washing the blade to avoid injuries.
4. Using the same solution as in step # 2, wipe clean the base of the blender.
5. Submerge cup, lid and blade assembly in a solution of sanitizer D10 suma bac. 20ml in 1ltr water.
6. Allow to air dry and reassemble.

Approved by: ____________ Issued by: ____________ Issue No. 01

Date: __________ Designation: __________ Checked by: __________

Date: ____________ Revision No. ____________

SOP No. 22: CLEANING OF MEAT MINCER

Objective: To stop bacterial growth and cross contamination.

Frequency: After every shift.

Supplies Required:

Chemical Required: D2.3l sumac multi, D10 suma bac (Johnson Diversey).

Responsibility: Line staff, shift supervisor and kitchen stewarding manager.

Procedure:

1. Disconnect electrical power from the unit to avoid accident.
2. Remove the cover and the cutter roll assembly.
3. Scrub lid and cutter roll assembly in hot water with D2.3l sumac multi solution.
4. Rinse with tap water and sanitize by dipping in sanitizing D10 suma bac solution.
5. Allow to air dry and reassemble when fully dried.

Approved by: ____________ Issued by: ____________ Issue No. 01

Date: __________ Designation: __________ Checked by: __________

Date: ____________ Revision No. ____________

SOP No. 23: CLEANING OF MEAT AND FOOD SLICER

Objective: To stop bacterial growth and cross contamination.

Frequency: After each use.

Chemical Required: D2.3l sumac multi, D10 suma bac (Johnson Diversey).

Responsibility: Line staff, shift supervisor and kitchen stewarding manager.

Procedure:

1. Always disconnect the electrical cord before starting to clean the slicer.
2. Set blade control at 0 t reduce the possibility of accidental cuts.
3. Leave the knife guard in place until ready to clean the knife. Then replace the guard as soon as the blade and guard are cleaned.
4. Clean the shafts and all parts under the frame.
5. Dismantle and remove parts to pot sink. Wash parts in a hot D2.3 suma multi solution.
6. Rinse with clear water.
7. Sanitize all removable parts and the blade in D10 suma bac sanitizing solution.

Approved by: ____________ Issued by: ____________ Issue No. 01

Date: __________ Designation: __________ Checked by: __________

Date: ____________ Revision No. ____________

SOP No. 24 : CLEANING OF STAINLESS STEEL SHELVING-COUNTERS AND TABLE

Objective: To reduce bacterial growth and cross contamination.

Scope: In all kitchen and service work areas.

Supplies Required: Scotch brite, dry Cloth.

Chemical Required: With D2.2 suma extra/D2.3l suma multi, D10 suma bac (Johnson Diversey).

Responsibility: Line staff, shift supervisor and kitchen stewarding manager.

Procedure:

1. Wipe up spilled or splashed food.
2. Clean the table tops, legs, sideways with D2.2 suma extra/ D2.3l suma multi solution. (20ml in 1ltr water) scrub with scotch brite.
3. Rinse it with clear hot water.
4. Santize with D10 suma bac sanitizing solution and let it air dry.

Approved by:______________Issued by:______________Issue No. 01

Date:___________Designation:___________Checked by:___________

Date:______________ Revision No.______________

SOP No. 25: CLEANING OF ICE MAKING MACHINE

Objective: To reduce bacterial growth and odor.
Frequency: Monthly.
Supplies Required: Scotch brite, dry cloth, hand brush.
Chemical Required: with D2.2 suma extra/D2.3l suma multi , D10 suma bac (Johnson Diversey).
Responsibility: Line staff, shift supervisor and kitchen manager.

Procedure:

Deliming

1. Using a warm solution of D9 suma scale of 33 per cent strength, brush wash all of the machine, inside and out, using a nylon bristled brush.
2. Make sure holes in water control are completely cleaned so as to give an even flow of water down over freezing board.
3. Rinse thoroughly with D10 suma bac sanitizer and reassemble machine for operation.
4. Clean the exterior with a warm solution D2.2 suma extra/ D2.3l suma multi.
5. Rinse with clear water and wipe dry.

Approved by:____________Issued by:____________Issue No. 01

Date:__________Designation:__________Checked by:__________

Date:____________ Revision No.____________

SOP No. 26: CLEANING OF WALK-IN REFRIGERATORS-FREEZER

Objective: To reduce bacterial growth and odor.
Frequency: Daily, weekly.
Scope: All kitchen and stores walk-in refrigerators shall be covered in this SOP.
Supplies Required: Scotch brite, dry cloth, hand brush, floor brush, squeezer, kent key mop.
Chemical Required: D2.2 suma extra/D2.3l suma multi, D10 suma bac. (Johnson Diversey).
Responsibility: Line staff, shift supervisor and kitchen stewarding manager.

Procedure:

Daily

1. Wipe up spilled liquids immediately so that they will not make cleaning more difficult and create unnecessary hazards.
2. Pick up scraps and particles and damp mop the floor with a warm solution of sanitizer.

Note: Do not damp mop freezers.

Weekly

1. Remove contents of the box to protected storage.
2. If cleaning freezer, adjust temperature control to above freezing (32°F)
3. Apply a warm solution of D2.2 suma extra/D2.3l suma multi to all surfaces
4. Scrub shelves, braces, hooks, walls and floors to remove stubborn soil.
5. Rinse with clear water.
6. Sanitize-saturate the entire shelving area, walls, ceiling and floor with a warm solution of sanitizer D10 suma bac. Let it dry.
7. Return food to the refrigerator/ freezer and adjust temperature controls back to normal setting.

Approved by: ____________ Issued by: ____________ Issue No. 01

Date: __________ Designation: __________ Checked by: __________

Date: ____________ Revision No. ____________

SOP No. 27: CLEANING OF REFRIGERATORS-REACH-IN

Objective: To reduce bacterial growth and odor.
Frequency: Every night.
Scope: All food and beverage production areas stores and receiving shall be covered in this SOP.
Supplies Required:
Chemical Required: D2.2 suma extra/D2.3l suma multi, D10 suma bac (Johnson Diversey).
Responsibility: Line staff, shift supervisor and kitchen stewarding manager.

Procedure:

*Remove all food stuff to protected temporary storage.

Interior Shelving

1. Remove shelving and loose equipment pot and pan sink.
2. Wash in a hot solution of D2.2 suma extra/D2.3l suma multi.
3. Rinse with clear water.
4. Sanitize-put shelving and equipments into a sanitizing rinse solution of D10 suma bac in the rinse tank.

Interior of Box

1. Wash interior with a warm solution of D10 suma bac sanitizer. Give special attention the floor the box, corners, doors, openings, gaskets, hinges and latches.
2. Sanitize interior with above mention solution and allow to air dry.
3. Return the shelving and food stuff to the box.

Exterior

1. Wipe down all heavily soiled exterior surfaces with a warm solution of D2.2 suma extra /D2.3l suma multi. Wipe dry with a clean cloth.
2. For stainless steel or aluminium exteriors, wipe and polish with a clean, dry cloth.

Approved by: ____________ Issued by: ____________ Issue No. 01

Date: __________ Designation: __________ Checked by: __________

Date: ____________ Revision No. ____________

SOP No. 28: CLEANING OF FOOD CARTS

Objective: To reduce bacterial growth and odor.

Scope: All f&b production areas stores and receiving shall be covered in this SOP. It shall include all kitchens, receiving, store and butchery carts in this SOP.

Frequency:

Supplies Required: Hand brush, scotch brite, duster.

Chemical Required: D10 suma bac (Johnson Diversey).

Responsibility: Line staff, shift supervisor and kitchen stewarding manager.

Procedure:

1. Brush or wipe off all loose soil. Clean out corners.
2. Make a mixer of D10 suma bac (20ml in 1ltr water for normal soiling, 50 ml in 1ltr water for heavy soiling) in a big container heat this mixer.
3. Put the crate into this solution one by one for 3 to 5 mnt.
4. Scrub with a nylon hand brush from in side and outside.
5. Stack all the crates and keep them dry in the air.

Deliming (Stainless Steel Carts only)

1. Should water spots, streaks or dulling lime appear on the carts, apply a solution of D5.2 suma scale 33 per cent strength. Allow solution to soak until haze or streaks are removed.
2. Rinse with clear water and wipe dry.

Approved by: ____________ Issued by: ____________ Issue No. 01

Date: __________ Designation: __________ Checked by: __________

Date: ____________ Revision No. ____________

SOP No. 29: CLEANING AND SANITIZING OF CHOPPING BOARDS

Objective: To reduce bacterial growth.
Frequency: Weekly, as per schedule.
Supplies Required: Hand brush, chopping board scrubber.
Chemical Required: D9 suma grill (Johnson Diversey).
Responsibility: Line staff, shift supervisor and kitchen stewarding manager.

Procedure:

1. Brush all loose soil from the surfaces with hand brush.
2. Make a solution with D9 suma grill in a big pot heat this solution.
3. Put chopping boards in to the solution for 10 to 15 mnts. Scrub with a stiff bristled brush or scrub with chopping board scrubber.
4. Rinse with D10 suma bac sanitizing solution.
5. Let air dry.

Approved by: ____________Issued by:____________Issue No. 01

Date: __________Designation: __________Checked by:__________

Date: ____________ Revision No. ____________

SOP No. 30: CLEANING OF GARBAGE BINS

Objective: To reduce bacterial growth.
Supplies Required: Hand brush, bucket, water.
Chemical Required: D2.2 suma extra/D2.3l suma multi, D10 suma bac (Johnson Diversey).
Responsibility: Line staff, shift supervisor and kitchen stewarding manager.

Procedure:

1. Bursh wash all heavily soiled garbage cans with a hot solution of D2.2 suma extra /D2.3 L suma multi.
2. Hose down all garbage cans, buckets and garbage disposable containers with hot water.
3. Rinse it with D10 suma bac solution for sanitizing.
4. Let it air dry.

Approved by: ____________ Issued by: ____________ Issue No. 01

Date: __________ Designation: __________ Checked by: __________

Date: ____________ Revision No. ____________

SOP No. 31: CLEANING OF DISHWASHING MACHINE

Objective: To reduce bacterial growth in service equipments.

Frequency: Hand brush, scotch brite, water.

Supplies Required:

Chemical Required: D5.2 suma scale, D10 suma bac (Johnson Diversey).

Responsibility: Line staff, shift supervisor and kitchen stewarding manager.

Procedure:

1. Turn off the machine, all heaters and electronic dispenser after the dishwashing operations are over.
2. Remove and clean curtains by scrubbing with D5.2 suma scale and water. Inspect curtains to make sure they are in good condition.
3. Remove and clean scrap trays. Clean out pump screens.
4. Remove and clean the wash and power rinse arms. Clean final rinse jets by poking out obstructions.
5. Flush out inside of the machine with hot water hose and sanitize with D10 suma bac solution.
6. Clean top and sides of machine. Scrub all work tables with detergent and water. Rinse and squeeze dry.
7. Clean walls and floor with detergent and water.

Approved by:____________ Issued by:____________ Issue No. 01

Date:__________ Designation: __________ Checked by:__________

Date: ____________ Revision No. ____________

SOP No. 32: CLEANING OF EXHAUST HOODS AND FILTER

Objective: To avoid fire hazards and reduce the smoke level in food production areas.

Supplies Required: Hand brush, scotch brite, water.

Chemical Required: D9 suma grill (Johnson Diversey).

Responsibility: Line staff, shift supervisor and kitchen stewarding manager.

Procedure:

Filters

1. Take out filters form hoods and take them to washing area. (behind garbage room)
2. Spray hot water on them to remove excess oil and dust.
3. Make a solution of D9 suma grill in boiling water in a large stainless steel container.
4. Dip the filters for soaking in grill solution till the grease comes out completely.
5. Take out the filters from the solution.
6. Spray hot water with the help of hose pipe/ pressure washer.
7. Scrub the filters with abrasive pads and a warm solution of light foaming soap.
8. Rinse well with clear hot water.
9. Shake of excess water and wipe with a clean cloth and allow to air dry.

Hoods

1. Clean the all surfaces of hoods with a cloth/duster to remove dust.
2. Apply a warm solution of D9 suma grill on all the surfaces for soaking. (inside and outside)
3. Scrub all the surfaces with abrasive pad thoroughly and wipe all the surfaces with cloth.
4. Pay special attention to the drainages, remove grease with the help of hot solution of Grill. Scrub it with stiff bristled brush and take out all the grease with damp cloth.
5. Spray a warm solution of light foaming soap, scrub all the surfaces with abrasive pad.
6. Wipe with damp cloth.

Approved by: ____________Issued by:____________Issue No. 01

Date: __________Designation: __________Checked by:__________

Date: ____________ Revision No. ____________

SOP No 33: DELIMING OF WATER BOILER

Objective: To remove lime scale from boiler.
Supplies Required: Hand brush, dry cloth.
Chemical Required: D5.2 suma (Johnson Diversey)
Responsibility: Line staff, shift supervisor and kitchen stewarding manager.

Procedure:

1. Fill the water in the boiler at the above the scale marks.
2. Heat up the boiler till 180 degree F, turn off the boiler, unplug from electrical connections.
3. Add D5.2 suma scale of 33 per cent strength in the hot water of boiler.
4. Leave the boiler for 1-2 hrs.
5. Flush the D5.2 suma scale solution from the boiler.
6. Rinse with clear hot water.
7. Take a warm solution of light foaming soap, apply on inner surface of boiler and scrub with a stiff bristled brush thoroughly.
8. Ensure that no lime scale marks is left.
9. Rinse thoroughly with clear hot water.
10. Wipe with clean, dry cloth.

Approved by: ____________ Issued by: ____________ Issue No. 01

Date: __________ Designation: __________ Checked by: __________

Date: ____________ Revision No. ____________

SOP No. 34: DISH WASHING OF EQUIPMENTS

(Through Dishwashing Machine
Three Stage Cleaning)

Objective: This is very important process to wash the Crockery, Cutlery, Glasses.
In hygienic manner to avoid any kind of bacterial hazard to the guest.

Supplies Required: Sponge, scotch brite, dry cloth.

Chemical Required: Sumac nova, suma rinse (these chemicals are dispensing through dozing pumps attached with dish washer), D2.2 suma extra/D2.3l suma multi and vim powder. (Johnson Diversey)

Responsibility: Line staff, shift supervisor and kitchen stewarding manager.

Procedure:

1. Outlet staff comes and stacked in individual racks Dinner Plates, Dessert Plates, Cutlery and Glassware and put in soaking bins all other items.
2. Each item is then pre washed manually at the sink with D2.2 suma extra /D2.3l suma multi.
3. These are then put in dish wash racks and pass through the Dishwashing Machine which has three stages.

   Stage-A –Pre Wash

   In this stage jets of luck warm water spread from the top and from the bottom.

   Stage-B–Wash

   In this stage soap solution jets hits the equipments from the top and the bottom.

   Stage-C–Rinse

   Here hot water and Rinse Aid mixture hit the equipments to rinse the washed and cleaned equipments to get rid of any traces of soap let on the equipments.
4. Next these washed and cleaned equipments are allowed to

rest for a while in their racks to shake off the excess water if any.

5. These items then wiped and kept ready for use.

Approved by:_____________Issued by:_____________Issue No. 01

Date:__________Designation:__________Checked by:__________

Date:_____________ Revision No._____________

SOP No. 35: POT WASHING OF EQUIPMENTS

Objective: This is very important process to wash the pots and pans and other food. Production equipments to stop contamination and bacterial growth. In food production equipments, to avoid any kind of food hazards.

Supplies Required: Sponge, scotch brite, hand brush, water.

Chemical Required: D2.2 suma extra/D2.3l suma multi (Johnson Diversey).

Responsibility: Line staff, shift supervisor and kitchen stewarding manager.

Procedure:

1. Kitchen staff comes and place the soiled utensils, pots and pans at pot wash area, which is located beside the kitchen.
2. Pot washer than emptied out the left over food if any with hand brush in wet garbage bins, then put in the pre soaking sink (first sink) to loosened the dirties from the equipments.
3. Then scrub the pots and pans with scotch pads/sponges/ brush to remove the food particles from utensils with D2.2 suma extra/D2.3l suma multi and vim powder.
4. Rinse well in running water, in second sink.
5. Ensure that no food dirties/greasiness on the utensils is left.
6. Stacked/store up side down on pot washing racks for next use.

Approved by: __________ Issued by: __________ Issue No. 01

Date: __________ Designation: __________ Checked by: __________

Date: __________ Revision No. __________

SOP No. 36: CLEANING OF WALK-IN REFRIGERATORS-FREEZER AND DEEP FREEZER

Objective: To reduce bacterial growth and odor.

Frequency: Daily, weekly.

Scope: All kitchen and butchery stores walk-in refrigerators shall be covered in this SOP.

Supplies Required: Scotch brite, dry cloth, hand brush, floor brush, squeezer, kent key mop.

Chemical Required: D2.2 suma extra/D2.3l suma multi, D10 suma bac.

Responsibility: Line staff, shift supervisor and kitchen stewarding manager.

Procedure:

Daily

1. Wipe up spilled liquids immediately so that they will not make cleaning more difficult and create unnecessary hazards.
2. Pick up scraps and particles and damp mop the floor with a warm solution of sanitizer.

Note:

1. Do not damp mop freezers.
2. For deep freezer cleaning defreeze the deep freezer.

Weekly

1. Remove contents of the box to protected storage.
2. If cleaning freezer, adjust temperature control to above freezing (32°F).
3. Apply a warm solution of D2.2 suma extra /D2.3l suma multi to all surfaces
4. Scrub shelves, races, hooks, walls and floors to remove stubborn soil.
5. Rinse with clear water.
6. Sanitize-saturate the entire shelving area, walls, ceiling and floor with a warm solution of Sanitizer D10 suma bac. Let it dry.
7. Return food to the refrigerator/ freezer and adjust temperature controls back to normal setting.

Approved by: ____________ Issued by: ____________ Issue No. 01

Date: __________ Designation: __________ Checked by: __________

Date: ____________ Revision No. ____________

SOP No. 37: CLEANING OF FOOD CARTS

Objective: To reduce bacterial growth and odor.

Scope: All food and beverage production areas stores and receiving shall be covered in this SOP.

It shall include all kitchens, receiving, store and butchery weighing scale in this SOP.

Supplies Required: Hand brush, spray bottle, scotch brite duster.

Chemical Required: D10 suma bac (Johnson Diversey).

Responsibility: Line staff, shift supervisor and kitchen stewarding manager.

Procedure:

1. Brush or wipe off all loose soil. Clean out corners of weighing scale.
2. Make a mixer of D10 suma bac (20ml in 1 ltr water for normal soiling, 50 ml in 1 ltr water for heavy soiling) in a spray bottle.
3. Spray this solution on weighing scale.
4. Scrub with a nylon hand brush.
5. Clean with a dry cloth.

Approved by: ____________ Issued by: ____________ Issue No. 01

Date: __________ Designation: __________ Checked by: __________

Date: ____________ Revision No. ___________

SOP No. 38: SETUP OF DISHWASHING MACHINE

Check the machine is clean from inside and outside.

From Inside:

- Wash arm are clean and properly fixed.
- Scrapped tray are cleaned and are in their proper place.
- Final rinse jets are cleaned and properly fixed.
- Curtains are cleaned properly and are in proper place in the machine.
- Check and close drain valves tightly.
- Open fill valves and fill water in the tank up to drain valve level.
- Shut off all fill vales of the tank.
- Close the machine shutters.
- Switch on the ON/OFF switch of the machine.
- Switch on the electric steam heater for all the tanks and final rinkse tank.
- Check and be sure rinse bottles and soap dispenser is filled up. Replace or fill, if necessary.
- Turn on all the dishwashing motors.
- Turn on all the soap and rinse dispensers.
- Check the temperature of the machine.
- Temperatures:
  Pre-wash Tank: 55°C
  Wash Tank: 70°C
  Final Rinse: 82°C

Approved by: ____________ Issued by: ____________ Issue No. 01

Date: __________ Designation: __________ Checked by: __________

Date: ____________ Revision No. ____________

SOP No. 39: OPERATION OF DISHWASHING MACHINE

- Place dishes of same size together in dishwashing machine rack.
- Place dish in a straight row.
- Do not overload or overlap plates in the rack.
- Put the loaded rack in the dishwashing machine.

Approved by: ____________Issued by:____________Issue No. 01

Date: __________Designation: __________Checked by:__________

Date: ____________ Revision No. ____________

SOP No. 40: CLEAN DISH HANDLING

- When the rack comes out of the machine allow dish to drain and air dried 20 to 25 seconds.
- Tilt cups, glasses and bowl racks to drain excess water from recessed bottom.
- Remove clean dishes from the rack. Stack them on their storing places.
- Take out any dirty and tarnished chinaware and cutlery and pre-soak in their respective tanks.
- Change water in all tanks after every four hours of using the machine.
- Change presoak water when it becomes dirty.

Approved by: ____________Issued by:____________Issue No. 01

Date: __________Designation: __________Checked by:__________

Date: ____________ Revision No. ____________

SOP No. 41: CLEANING OF DISHWASHING MACHINE

- Switch off all heaters, soap dispensers and rinse dispensers of the machine.
- Remove all the curtains.
- Clean the curtains with soap solution and water.
- Inspect curtains that they are not torn, if so, please notify to you supervisor on duty.
- Let air dried the curtains.
- Removed scrapped tray and clean with soap solutions and hot water.
- Remove wash and power rinse arms and clean with soap solution and hot water.
- Clean final rinse jets by poking out obstructions.
- Drain out water of all the tanks.
- Clean tanks from inside with soap solutions and hot water.
- Clean top and sides of the machine with soap solution and with hot water.
- Reassemble the machine.
- Scrub all the work tables with soap solution and with hot water
- Rinse and squeeze dry.
- Clean wall and floors of dishwashing area with soap solutions and water.

Approved by: ____________ Issued by: ____________ Issue No. 01

Date: __________ Designation: __________ Checked by: ________

Date: ____________ Revision No. ___________

SOP No. 42: BUSSING DISHES AND LOADING THE DISH MACHINE

- Set up a silver pre-soak pan on the soiled dish table use a stainless steel pan. Put a place of aluminium foil in the bottom, add hot water and TOWER change the solution when it becomes dirty.
- Place glass, cup, and bowl racks on the overhead shelf. Make sure that these items are placed in each compartment upside down.
- Set out decoys on the tables so that the bus boys and bus girls can place dish all of one kind together.
- Always knock off excess food soil and paper before racking dishes so that heavy food particles do not enter the wash tank.
- Rack dishes, all of one kind, together. Then rinse with overhead spray to knock off any remaining heavy food soil.
- Rack silver in holders with eating and up. Do not place same kind together or they will nest and not wash thoroughly.

Approved by: __________Issued by:__________Issue No. 01

Date:__________Designation: __________Checked by:__________

Date: __________ Revision No. __________

SOP No. 43: RECOMMENDED WAREWASHING PROCEDURES

Daily procedures to clean up dishwashing machine.

Clean Dish Handling

1. Allow dishes to drain and air dry for several seconds after leaving machine. Tilt cup and glass rack to drain excess water from recessed bottoms.
2. Remove clean dishes from rack and stack them in their proper storage places.
3. Check to see flatware is clean and dry. Sort and store them. Any dirty or tarnished flatware should be re-soaked and rewashed.

Clean Up

4. Turn off machine, all heaters, and electronic dispenser. Remove and clean curtains by scrubbing with detergent and water. Inspect curtains to make sure they are in good condition.
5. Remove and clean scrap tray. Clean out pump screens. Check and clean overflows.
6. Remove and clean out wash and power rinse arms. Clean final rinse jet by poking out obstructions.
7. Flesh out inside of machine with hose. If possible, use a GUN-SPRAY with a detergent sanitizer.
8. Clean top and sides of machine. Scrub all worktable with detergent and water. Rinse and Squeegee dry.
9. Clean walls and floor with detergent an water. If possible, use a GUN-SPRAY with a detergent sanitizer.

Approved by: ____________Issued by:____________Issue No. 01

Date:__________Designation: __________Checked by:__________

Date: ____________ Revision No. ____________

SOP No. 44: RUGRAD SERVICE

Trouble Shooter

It simple checks for mechanical dishwashing operations….. "fist aids" for curing daily problems:

Trouble	Check	Why
1. Scale in the	(a) Water hardness	(a) Water will deposit temporary hardness when heated. Excessively hard rinse water should be softened.
	(b) Detergent concentrations	(b) Properly built detergents will control water hardness if used at recommended concentrations.
	(c) Daily cleanup	(c) Daily maintenance will keep machine clean. The compound used from machine dishwashing may also be used for this cleaning job.
2. Grease film in machine and on dishes	(a) Daily cleanup	(a) Some areas not contacted by detergent sprays will show fil. Scrub these areas and other soil fill. Scrub these areas and other soil from red positing on machine walls.
	(b) Detergent concentrations	(b) A properly maintained solution will have a soil tolerance capable of keeping grease and other soil from red positing on machine walls.
	(c) Fresh water addition to wash tank	(c) Wash tank should be continuously replenished with fresh water to allow surface scum to overflow to the dram. Too much overflow reduces wash water concentrations.
3. Water sport and films on dishes and glasses	(a) Final rinse jets	(a) Final rinse removes wash water. Coverage must be adequate.
	(b) Hardness of rinse water	(b) Water will deposited temporary hardness when heated.
	(c) Time temperature and pressure of rinse	(c) Time-too short-leaves soil. Temperature too hot-causes flash drying, leaves sports pressure-too low-poor rinse. Too high-tends to fog.
	(d) Drying time	(d) If too long water remaining will cause sports. A rinse additive would be indicated to produce "sheeting off" of the rinse water to produce a dry dish.

Contd...

Trouble	Check	Why
		If rinse additive is being used do not overuse.
	(e) Insufficient use of detergent	(e) To control water hardness. Concentration must be maintained with a detergent having this ability.
4. Excessive foaming or sudsing	(a) Detergent	(a) Should not be of the sudsing type.
	(b) Rinse additive	(b) Rinse additive should be minimum sudsing.
	(c) Wash water level in wash tank	(c) Water in wash tank should always cover pump inlet. If not, pump will beat air in to the solution causing suds.
	(d) Fresh water additions to the wash tank	(d) Grease scum should overflow down the drain. Otherwise it will form suds.
	(e) Daily cleanup of machine	(e) Empty machine while still jot to prevent grease scum on sides of tank clean daily.
5. Grease films on dishes	(a) Detergent concentrations	(a) Proper concentration is necessary for cleaning.
	(b) Wash water temperatures	(b) 150-160°F, gives best result.
	(c) For clogged wash arms and pump action	(c) Must cause good scrubbing action.
	(d) For plugged rinse jets	(d) Rinse nozzles must be kept free from scale for good flooding effect.
6. "Dirty" dishes	(a) Wash sprays	(a) Low pressure or clogged wash sprays cause poor washing.
	(b) Insufficient detergent	(b) For good soil removal enough detergent must be used.
	(c) Overflows	(c) Grease should overflow from wash tank keeping wash water clean.
	(d) Rinse sprays	(d) Additions of fresh water to the wash tanks through fill valves or from rinse water are needed to cause overflow and keep wash water clean.
7. Black markings on dishes	(a) Racks and table	(a) Markings come from contact surfaces.
	(b) Rubber or plastic	(b) This can be corrected by daily Cleaning or covering.

Contd...

Trouble	*Check*	*Why*
8. Coffee stains	*(a)* Detergent concentration and type	*(a)* New detergents are available which remove stains from china and plastic ware and prevent stain formation through regular use in the dishwashing machine.
	(b) Washing time	*(b)* Adequate time is needed for stain removal.

Approved by:____________Issued by:____________Issue No. 01

Date:____________Designation:____________Checked by:____________

Date:____________ Revision No.____________

SOP No. 45: POTS AND PANS CLEANING

Three Tank Procedure

- Fill wash tank with hot water and add one cup with soap solution.
- Fill the rinse tank with clear and hot water.
- Fill sanitizing tank with warm water and add 4 oz. Chlorine in the water.
- Scrap off all the excess soil from pots and pans so as not to load the sink with soil.
- Throw the soil in the garbage drum.
- Place the scrapped utensil in the wash tank for soaking.
- Switch on the pots and pans motors and allow utensil to soak for 5 minutes. (if motor is insulted in area)
- Scrub the utensil from inside and outside surface with pot and pan brush or abrasive pad.
- Remove utensil from wash tank and allow wash solution to drain back in the wash tank.
- Completely submerge utensil in the rinse tank.
- Remove utensils from rinse tank and submerge in sanities tank sink.
- Retain the utensils in sanitized sink for one minute.
- Remove utensils from sanitized sink and place upside down in the rack and let air dried.
- Stack the utensils at their storage place.

Two Tank Procedurre

- Use sink number one for washing and sink number two for sanitizing rinse.
- In this case remove utensil from wash tank and flush or spray with clear water and then place in the sanitizing tank.

Cleaning of the Pot Washing Sink

- At the end of every work period.
- Fill the tank to low level with hot solution of liquid soap.
- Brush wash inside and outside of all tanks, the drain table and splash.
- Drain and rinse all tanks.
- Squeeze water from all flat surfaces.

Decaled the Sinks as Required

After the utensils have been cleaned in the usual manner, any mineral deposit or the fills should be removed by using a warm solution of descaling compound.

Approved by: ____________ Issued by: ____________ Issue No. 01

Date: __________ Designation: __________ Checked by: __________

Date: ____________ Revision No. __________

SOP No. 46: BAKE OVENS CLEANING

Interior

- Preheat oven to 150°F. (65° CENTIGRADE)
- Switch off the oven.
- Spray the interior with grease remover while surface are warm.
- Let the solution stand on soil for 4 to 5 minutes to permit chemical cleaning action to take place.
- Use a stiff brush/scrubber to remove the baked on grease or carbonized food soil.
- Use a damp cloth to pick up the dissolve and loosen soil.
- Let air dried.

Exterior

- Spray outside the oven with grease remover.
- Use a damp cloth to pick up the dissolve and loosen soil.
- Rinse with clear water.
- Wipe dry with the clean dry cloth.
- Keep the sides, front and back of the oven clean at all times.

Approved by: ____________Issued by:____________Issue No. 01

Date: __________Designation: __________Checked by:__________

Date: ____________ Revision No. ____________

SOP No. 47: HOT BAIN MARIE STAINLESS STEEL

- Turn off steam.
- Remove all containers of food.
- Open drain faucet and let all water drain out.
- Prepare soap solution in one pan.
- Fill second pan with rinse water.
- Brush wash all surface with hot solution of soap, e.g. top back, front and sides.
- Use a dull mattle scrubber to remove the baked or stubborn food.
- Rinse with hot water and wipe dry.

Periodic Descaling

- Fill steam well with water an add descaling powder/solution.
- Turn on the steam and allow hot solution to remain all lime scaling has been removed.
- Use light brush or scrubber to remove heavy lime scale.
- Turn off the steam, drain steam wells.
- Thoroughly brush with hot water.
- Wipe dry.

Approved by: ____________ Issued by: ____________ Issue No. 01

Date: __________ Designation: __________ Checked by: __________

Date: ____________ Revision No. ____________

SOP No. 48: BROILER CLEANING

- Let the broiler cool enough to handle.
- Take out all removable parts.
  A. Drip Pan.
  B. Racks.
- Take them to the pot washing fop soaking, scrubbing and follow the pots and pans washing procedure.

Interior

- Spray grease remover in the interior.
- Allow 5 minutes for solution to soak in and to soften the soil.
- Use stiff brush to remove the baked grease.
- Use a damp cloth to pick dissolved loosen grease.
- Rinse with clear are water and let air dry.
- Reassemble the drip pan and racks.

Exterior

- Spray outside of the unit with grease remover.
- Remover the loosed soil with dam cloth.
- Rinse with clear water.
- Wipe dry with clean and dry duster.

Important

BE SURE THAT THE ENTIRE EXTERIOR AREA UNDERNEATH AND BEHIND THE EQUIPMENT ARE CLEANED.

Approved by: ____________ Issued by: ____________ Issue No. 01

Date: __________ Designation: __________ Checked by: __________

Date: ____________ Revision No. ____________

SOP No. 49: GRILLS AND GRIDDLES CLEANING

- Scrape all loose soil from the surface as soon as equipment is cool enough to work.
- Spray grease remover on surface of the griddle when it is still warm.
- Allow it to penetrate the soil. Clean the edges and side of the griddle.
- Scrape off the loosened soil and rinse with a wet cloth.
- Empty the scraping pans.
- Clean it with the hot soap solution and replace it.
- Start the griddle to heat again.
- Brush with food grade vegetable oil.

Important

KEEP THE BASE OF GRIDDLE, THE TOP AND SIDES OF STAND, THE BACK PLATE AND THE PATTER SHEET THROUGHLY CLEAN AT ALL TIME.

Approved by:____________Issued by:____________Issue No. 01

Date:__________Designation:__________Checked by:__________

Date:____________ Revision No.____________

SOP No. 50: KETTLE STEAM JACKETED

Cleaning

- Remove the leftover food stuff from the kettle.
- Flush the kettle with warm water and allow to drain.
- Close valve and fill kettle with ½ full with hot water and add detergent.
- Brush scrub all surface inside and outside.
- Use small brush to clean the drain off pipes and outlet valves as the solution is draining.
- Scrap the adjacent piping, braces and valves.
- Clean the cover from outside and inside including power springs.
- Rinse all washed surfaces with hot water.

Approved by: __________ Issued by: __________ Issue No. 01

Date: __________ Designation: __________ Checked by: __________

Date: __________ Revision No. __________

SOP No. 51: DEEP FRYERS GAS CLEANING

- Allow deep fryer to cool.
- Filter the oil and transfer it to pre cleaned reservoir.
- Fill water into the deep well only to cover the heating coils.
- Add 2 per cent of detergent in the deep well.
- Thoroughly mixed this concentrated solution.
- Turn on the heat and bring the temperature to 180°F to 200°F. (90° CENTIGRADE).
- Allow coil to soak in this solution until completely cleaned.
- Fill up the deep well with hot water to required level.
- Bring the temperature to boiling.
- Brush wash any heavy deposits using the solution inside the deep well.
- Brush wash outside surface using the same solution.
- When the tank is completely cleaned, turn heat off and drain out the solution.
- Add cold water to the solution as it drains to prevent rapid change in temperature or cooling too rapidly.
- Rinse thoroughly with fresh water.

Approved by: ____________Issued by:____________Issue No. 01

Date: __________Designation: __________Checked by:__________

Date: ____________ Revision No. ____________

SOP No. 52: STACK OVEN CLEANING

Interior Spray Cleaning Procedure

- Preheat oven to 150°F. (65° CENTIGRADE).
- Switch off the oven.
- Spray the interiors with grease remover and let it soak in completely.
- Use a stiff brush/scrubber to loosen the baked on grease or carbonized food.
- Use a damp cloth to pick up the dissolved and loosen grease soil.
- Rinse with clear water.
- Let it air dry.

Metal Floor Inserts Cleaning

- Should be removed when they become stained.
- Prepare caustic soda solution in the sink.
- Switch on the steam to bring the temperature to 180°F.
- Submerge the inserts in the tank for 2 minutes.
- Turn the insert and scrap it both sides one by one.
- Rinse in clear water and let it air dry.
- Replace in oven.

Exterior Tray Decreasing Process

- Spray soiled surface with grease remover.
- Use stiff brush/scrubber to remove baked grease.
- Rinse with clear water.
- Let air dry.

Important

BE SURE THAT ENTIRE EXTERIOR ARE, UNDERNEATH AND BEHIND THE OVEN ARE THROUGHLY CLEANED.

Approved by: ____________ Issued by: ____________ Issue No. 01

Date: __________ Designation: __________ Checked by: __________

Date: ____________ Revision No. ____________

SOP No. 53: RANGES HOODS WITH REMOVABLE FILTERS CLEANING

- Switch on the steam for 15 minutes to loosened the grease.
- Remove filters from hood.
- Spray all surface, inside and out side hood with grease remover.
- Use brush to remove the backed grease until it is dissolved and loosened.
- Clean out drain trough around the lower inside edge of the hood as well as the channel which hold the filters.
- Clean and polish the exterior surface.

Approved by: ____________ Issued by: ____________ Issue No. 01

Date: __________ Designation: __________ Checked by: ________

Date: ____________ Revision No. ____________

SOP No. 54: DISHWASHING MACHINE METHOD

- Take the removed filters to the dishwashing machine after all the dishes washed for the day.
- Make sure that filter are not broken or worn-out, that will jam the dishwashing machine.
- Lay each through the full wash and rinse clean.
- Examine each filter as its comes out from the machine.
- If not thoroughly clean, run it through again.
- Stack filters on the drain board until dry.
- Replace filter in the hood.

Manual Cleaning Method

- Once a week remove the filter to the pot wash sink and soak in the hot solution of detergent/degreaser.
- Turn on the steam to boil the water (hotter the water, the faster the grease will be loosened from the filters).
- Remover the filter and flush thoroughly under hot water tap to remove cleaning solution and grease.
- Stack on drain board until dry.
- Replace filter in the hood.

Approved by: ____________ Issued by: ____________ Issue No. 01

Date: __________ Designation: __________ Checked by: __________

Date: ____________ Revision No. ____________

SOP No. 55: FOOD CHOPPER CLEANING

Dismantle and clean at the end of each use period as follows:

Caution

Disconnect the electric power and clean the blades with great care, to avoid accidents and injuries, leave the guard in place until the rest of the machine id clened. Remove guard only long enough to clean it and the blade. Use a brush with long handle.

- Disassembled parts should be taken to pot sink.
- Flush with tap water to remove loose soil.
- Wash these parts in a hot solution of liquid soap.
- Rinse thoroughly with clear water.
- Dip all parts in a sanitizing solution.
- Wipe clean all stationery components using the solution of liquid soap.
- Dry with clean duster.

Approved by: ____________ Issued by: ____________ Issue No. 01

Date: __________ Designation: __________ Checked by: __________

Date: ____________ Revision No. ____________

SOP No. 56: BLENDER CLEANING

Important

Disconnect the electrical power at the end of each use period.

- Remove the cup, lid and blade assembly.
- Wash in solution of liquid soap.
- Wipe clean the base of blender with the soap solution .
- Sumerge cup, lid and blade assemble in the sanitizing solution.
- Allow to air dry and reassemble.

Caution

Exercise care in washing the sharp blade to avoid injuries.

Approved by: ____________ Issued by: ____________ Issue No. 01

Date: __________ Designation: __________ Checked by: __________

Date: ____________ Revision No. ____________

SOP No. 57: MEAT MINCER CLEANING

Caution

Disconnect electric power from the unit to avoid accident.

- Remove the cover and cutter roll assembly.
- Brush meat scrap from cutter rolls.
- Scrub lid and cutter roll assembly in a hot solution of liquid soap.
- Rinse with tap water.
- Submerge in the sanitizing solution.
- Allow to air dry.
- Wipe clean all stationery parts with a warm sanitizing solution
- Reassemble the parts.

Approved by: ____________ Issued by: ____________ Issue No. 01

Date: __________ Designation: __________ Checked by: __________

Date: ____________ Revision No. ____________

SOP No. 58: POTATO PEELER CLEANING

Immediately After Use

- With peeler running, flush unit with cold water.
- DISCONNECT ELECTRIC POWER.
- Remove the lid abrasive discs, perforated strainer and stopper.
- Flush with cold water to clean the peel traps.
- Wash all removed parts in pot sink in a hot solution of liquid soap.
- Use long handle brush to wash inside and outside surfaces of the stationery unit with solution of liquid soap.
- Sanitize all parts by rinsing with a sanitizing solution.
- Reassemble all the parts.

Approved by: ____________ Issued by: ____________ Issue No. 01

Date: __________ Designation: __________ Checked by: __________

Date: ____________ Revision No. ____________

SOP No. 59: TOASTERS CLEANING

Important

Make certain that during the cleaning of operation, the electrical parts are not wet, as this could caused damage to the toaster or serious injury to the personnel when toaster again plugged in.

Pop-up Type

- Unplug.
- Unplug the toaster.

Interior

- Gently bump toaster on counter to knock all crumbs into the crumbs tray.
- Remove in clear water and dry with a clean duster.

Note: Do not attempt to clean the heating elements in any manner whatsoever.

Exterior

- Move toaster and wipe.
- Clean counter surface underneath.
- Wipe toaster with clean cloth and polish.
- Be careful not to get any of the solution inside the toaster.
- Polish with a clean dry cloth.
- Replace dry crumb tray.

Approved by:____________Issued by:____________Issue No. 01

Date:__________Designation: __________Checked by:__________

Date:____________ Revision No. ____________

SOP No. 60: TOASTER CONVEY OR TYPER

Interior

- Remove and empty crumb tray.
- Wipe crumb tray clean with a liquid soap.
- Rinse tray in clean with a liquid soap.

Note: Make no further attempt to clean interior of toaster.

Exterior

- Spray exterior or toaster with stainless steel polish and wipe dry.
- Move toaster and wipe clean the counter surface underneath.
- Wipe with clean dry cloth.
- Replace dry crumb tray.

Approved by: ____________Issued by:____________Issue No. 01

Date: __________Designation: __________Checked by:__________

Date: ____________ Revision No. ____________

SOP No. 61: MEAT AND FOOD SLICER CLEANING

After Each use Period

Caution

Always disconnect the electric cord before starting to clean the food slicer. Wet blade control at to reduce the possibility of accidental cuts.

Leave the knife guard in place until ready to clean the knife then replace the guard as soon as the blade and guard are cleaned.

Approved by: ____________Issued by:____________Issue No. 01

Date: __________Designation: __________Checked by:__________

Date: ____________ Revision No. ____________

SOP No. 62: CLEAN THE SHAFTS AND ALL PARTS UNDER THE FRAME

Cleaning

- Dismantle blade, wheel and frame.
- Remove the dismantle parts to pot sink
- Wash part in a hot solution of liquid soap.
- Rinse with clear water.
- Sanities it.
- Dip removable parts in a warm sanitizing solution.
- Clean the stationery parts in place with sanitizing solution be careful of the blade.
- Scrub with a long handle brush the sanitizing solution.
- Wipe the stationery parts with sanitizing solution.
- Let it air dry.

Approved by: ____________ Issued by: ____________ Issue No. 01

Date: __________ Designation: __________ Checked by: __________

Date: ____________ Revision No. ____________

SOP No. 63: CLEANING OF STAINLESS STEEL TABLE SHEVLES AND COUNTERS

- Wipe up spilled or splashed food
- Clean the to, legs ways with liquid soap solution.
- Scrub with steel-wool or scotch brite where it is rusty.
- Rinse with hot clear water.
- Sanitize with sanitizing solution.
- Let air dry.

Approved by: ____________ Issued by: ____________ Issue No. 01

Date: __________ Designation: __________ Checked by: __________

Date: ____________ Revision No. ____________

SOP No. 64: STAINLESS STEEL VEGETABLE SINKS WITH DRAIN BOARD

- At the end of each shift, scrub the entire sink, back splash, drain board, legs, supports and all exterior area with warm liquid soap solution.
- Rinse in with hot clean water.
- Sanitize it with sanitizing solution.
- Let it air dry.

Approved by: ______________Issued by:______________Issue No. 01

Date: ___________Designation: ___________Checked by:____________

Date: ______________ Revision No. ______________

SOP No. 65: PROOFING CABINET CLEANING

Cautions

The temperature and humidity conditions maintained in the proofing cabinet are ideal for bacteria and fungal growth. Therefore the cabinet must be cleaned carefully and sanitized to inhobit growth of these organish.

- Remove all food and trays from cabinets.
- Brush out all loose food particles soil.
- Steam the interior thoroughly.
- Sanitize it with sanitize solutions.
- Clean the exterior with sanitizing solution.
- Let air dry.

Approved by: ______________Issued by:______________Issue No. 01

Date: ___________Designation: ___________Checked by:____________

Date: ______________ Revision No. ______________

SOP No. 66: COFFEE MAKERS

Caution

Remove the electric pung from socket to avoid accident.

- Flush unit thoroughly with fresh water to remove loose soil.
- Remove cover brewing chamber, container and coffee container to pot sink for cleaning with a hot solution.
- Scrub the brew reservoir, parts gauges with liquid soap solution.
- Drain and flush thoroughly with clear hot water to remove all trace of the cleaning solution.

Exterior

- Wipe outside of the coffee maker with liquid soap solution.
- Wipe dry and polish with clean dry duster.

Coffee Urn *(Large Coffee Maker)*

Should be cleaned every evening.

Interior

- Close steam valve and drain out all coffee.
- Put 5 litres of clean hot water into the run.
- Brush the side with brush.
- Drain the water and rinse again by pouring hot water down over sides of interior.
- Drain all rinse water from the urn.
- Close the valve and pour in 21/2 liters of clean water.
- Leave this water in the run until ready to start a new batch of coffee.

Exterior

- Spray liquid soap solution at outside of run.
- Wipe dry and polish with a clean dry duster.

Descaling of Coffee URN

Once a Week

- Fill the water jacket to just above the scale line.
- Add descaling compound.
- Bring temperature up to 160°F.(70° Centigrade)
- Turn off heat and allow to stand one to two hours.

- Drain brushes the water jacket while it is draining to remove the softened scale.
- Rinse thoroughly with clean water.

Coffee and Tea Dispensers

- Empty the container
- Flush thoroughly with clean water.
- Scrub thoroughly with clean water.
- Be sure to dismantle and carefully clean the faucet each time they avoid is cleaned to avoid accumulation deposits.
- Rinse thoroughly with fresh water and invert to air dry.

Approved by: ____________ Issued by: ____________ Issue No. 01

Date: __________ Designation: __________ Checked by: __________

Date: ____________ Revision No. ____________

SOP No. 67: CLEANING OF ICE MACHINE

- Empty the ice machine.
- Brush wash ice machine all parts with decaling compound.
- Use a good nylon bristled brush.
- Use the same brush for cleaning inside and outside the machine.
- Make sure holes in water control are compactly cleaned so as to give an even flow of water down over freezing board.
- Rinse thoroughly with sanitizing solution.
- Reassemble machine for operation.

Exterior

- Clean all heavily soiled surfaces with a warm solution of liquid soap.
- Rinse with clean water.
- Wipe dry.
- Spray stainless steel surface with stainless steel cleaner.
- Wipe dry and polish with a clean dry cloth.

Approved by: ____________ Issued by: __________ Issue No. 01

Date: ______ Designation: _________ Checked by: _________

Date: ____________ Revision No. ___________

SOP No. 68: REFREIGRATER REACH-IN

- Remove all food stuff to protected temporary storage.
- Interior shelving.
- Remove shelving and loose equipment to pot and pan sink.
- Wash in a hot solution of liquid soap.
- Rinse with clear water.

Sanitize

Put shelving and equipment into a sanitizing rinse solution in the rinse tank.

Interior of Box

- Wash interior with a warm sanitizing solution.
- Clear floor of box , cornors, doors, openings, gaskets, hinges and latches with special attention.
- Let air dry.
- Replace the shelving and food stuffs to the box.

Exteriors

- Wipe down all heavily soiled exterior with warm soap solution.
- Wipe dry with a clean cloth.
- Clean stainless steel/aluminium with stainless steel cleaner.
- Wipe and polish with a clean dry cloth.

Approved by: ____________ Issued by: ____________ Issue No. 01

Date: __________ Designation: __________ Checked by: __________

Date: ____________ Revision No. ____________

SOP No. 69: FOOD CARTS-TRAY CART AND FOOD SERVICE TROLLIER

- Remove the food stuff/trays from cart.
- Brush or wipe off all soil.
- Clean out all the corners.
- Spray clean with sanitizing solution.
- Clean under shelves.
- Clean the wheels with brush.
- Get the wheels with brush.
- Rinse with clean water and wipe and wipe dry.

Approved by: ____________ Issued by: ____________ Issue No. 01

Date: __________ Designation: __________ Checked by: __________

Date: ____________ Revision No. ____________

SOP No. 70: ROOM SERVICE TROLLIERS AND HOT CASES

- Remove hot case from room service trolleys, if loaded.
- Clean the leg, wheel with soap solution.
- Clean the wheels with brush.
- Sanitize the stainless steel portion with sanitizing solution.
- Let air dry.
- Get the wheel lubricated required.

Approved by: ____________ Issued by: ____________ Issue No. 01

Date: __________ Designation: __________ Checked by: __________

Date: ____________ Revision No. ____________

SOP No. 71: CLEANING OF THE HOT CASE

Caution

Do not pour water on element.

- Remove the electrical plug if plugged in.
- Remove shelves from the hot case.
- Clean with soap solution using scotch brite.
- Rinse with hot clean water.
- Sanitize it with sanitizing solution.
- Wipe the hot case from outside and inside with soap solution.
- Sanitize it with sanitizing solution.
- Let air dry.
- Fix the shelves.

Approved by: ____________ Issued by: ____________ Issue No. 01

Date: __________ Designation: __________ Checked by: __________

Date: ____________ Revision No. ____________

SOP No. 72: CAN OPENERS

- Remove the opener by lifting the shank out of the base.
- Soak the shank assembly in the pot sink in a hot solution of liquid soap.
- Scrub all parts with a stiff bristle brush.
- Clean the blade and can holding mechanism with great attention.
- Rinse with clear water and sanitizing solution.
- Scrub the base using same sanitizing solution.
- Lubricate regularly.

Periodically

Remove the base from mounting if mounted.

- Clean and sanitize in sanitize solution.

Approved By: ____________ Issued By: ____________ Issue No. 01

Date: __________ Designation: __________ Cheked by __________

Date: ____________ Revision No. ____________

SOP No. 73: CLEANING OF CHOPPING BOARD, SANDWICH BOARD, CHEESE BOARD AND SALAD BOARD

- Cleaning sanitizing and deodorizing.
- Brush all loose soil from the surfaces.
- Wet the surface with warm water sprinkle with sanitizing in addition to cleaning and sanitizing. Sanitizing solution has good bleaching action.
- Scrub with stiff bristle brush dipper frequently in warm water of sanitizing solution.
- Rinse with warm water.
- Let it air dry.

Approved by: ____________Issued by:____________Issue No. 01

Date: __________Designation: __________Checked by:_________

Date: ____________ Revision No. ____________

SOP No. 74: BURNISHING SILVERWARE

Why?

Through the normal course of handling and use, silverware develops scratches and mars nits surface. This surface roughness diminishes the luster and fine appearance of the silver.

Caution

Always detarnish and clean silver before burnishing it. Burnishing fork together, knives together and spoon together. Do Not Mix.

Assemble all the clean silver that require burnishing.

- Remove the cover of burnishing solution tank and check if solution water is clean if not.
- Change the water after draining out of the used solution . Close the lid of water tank.
- Switch on burnishing rnachine and pour burnishing powder on burnishing bowls slowly.
- Let the machine operate 5 minutes to mix the burnishing powder.
- Put one kind of silverware in the burnishing machine tank where burnishing bowls are vibrating/rotating.

- Run the machine for 10 minutes longer. If the silver was badly scarred.
- Remove the silverware from burnishing machine, rinse and immediately pass through the dishwashing machine.
- Wipe the silverware with dry clean cloth.

Note

Burnishing solution should be change after every 10 to 12 cycles.

Deternishing Silverware, Presoaking

- Prepare a solution of deternishing compound in hot water.
- Submerge a sheet of Aluminium foil which completely covers the bottom of the mobile sink.
- Place the silver into the solution on top of the Aluminium foil 10-20 minutes before washing.
- Remove silverware directly from solution to flat racks.
- Spry rinse and immediately put through dishwashing machine.
- Wipe silverware with dry clean cloth.

Preparation of Deternishing Solution

Note

If the Deternishing solution not available then prepare this solution to use:

- Take S/S or plastic tub.
- Place silver foil at the bottom of the sink.
- Fill with hot water.
- Add 10gm of iodized salt.
- Add lemon peels or lemon juice.
- Add one table spoon of caustic soda.
- (SOLUTION IS READY TO USE)
- Submerge the silver in the sink/tub for 10 minutes.
- Remove the silver, wash and do burnishing. (Procedure as stated)

Approved by: ____________ Issued by: ____________ Issue No. 01

Date: __________ Designation: __________ Checked by: __________

Date: ____________ Revision No. ____________

SOP No. 75: DISH HANDLING–SOME RIGHT AND WRONG HAITS

- DO: Place the soiled dishes and glassware on the soiled dish table grouped according to size and type, following the decoy systems.
- Place cups and glassware in overhead racks where they are available.
- Scrape all loose soil from dishes before they are placed in racks or on the conveyor.
- Place dishes, cups and glassware in their proper racks and in such a way as to expose all the.
- Tableware to the cleaning and rinsing sprays.
  (Follow the manufacturer's and the detergent supplier's recommendations with regard to time, temperature and supplies used in the dishwashing machine.)
- DON'T: Place soiled tableware on to the dish table at random.
- "Throw" the tableware onto the soiled dish table.
- Put dishes with loose soild on them through the machine.
- Neglect to watch the water temperature in the dish machine.
- Mix such items as linen, bottles can etc. in bus boxes with china, glass or silver.

Silver Planting Process

Plain Bronze item can be transformed into a shiny silver item by electro plating and epns can be replated if the silver coating is torn off:

Plating of Bronze Item

Wash the item with fresh water of remove any dust deposit on it.

Tie the item with copper wire from one side and other side with the negative pole (Cathode) to immresed in the solution of silver potassium cyanide.

In the tank their is another pole which is positive (Anode) Pole: Silver plastec are attached to this pole.

Pass a low votage electric current through the circuit.

Silver atoms in the silver plate loose some of their electrons, flow into silver potassium cyanide and become positively charged silver ions ($Ag+$).

These ions are attracted to the negative pole, where they bond with electrons and reverts to silver atom and accumulate on the bronze item.

Bronze is silver plated on silver atom plate at a time.

Silver Melting Process

We purchase silver in strips 70 per cent thin and 30 per cent thick.

Withdraw silver from store on store requisition from.

Check the Accurate Weight of Silver

Cut the thin strips of silver in small pieces for melting and making solution for the tank.

Cut pieces of thick silver of approx 6-8" Size for hanging with a cathode rod.

Extraction of Grease

Blow the burner and put these strips in front of or on the burner to extract the grease.

Melting the Silver Strips

Put all small pieces of thin silver in a ceramic pot and add nitric acid (H No3) to Melt the silver strips.

Ag+Hno3 Silver Nitrate

Clarifying Process

Put sodium chloride (Salt) in Silver Nitrate

NaCl+Ag No3

It will become silver chloride.

Strain the water from the top and this process four to five time.

Now silver chloride is left

Add silver salt, potassium cyanide and copper connecting salt and connecting salt and put fire.

Connecting salt and put on fire.

It will become liquid and put the same in silver tank.

Silver Extracting Process

Take 75 per cent sulfuric acid (H2 SO4) in a steel container put 25 per cent of nitric acid (HN O3) and put on fire to boil it.

Add 10 per cent of water.

Now dip the silver platted equipment (from the silver is to be extracted) in the container. Silver will be extracted from brass.

Now put a copper strip or discarded copper equipment in the container copper will make the silver precipitated.

Take a muslin cloth to strain the silver residue.

Put container on file to evaporate the water.

Add salt peter in the silver and put in a crucible (kothali) made of graphite put on it to boil the silver residue.

Silver will come out.

Approved by: ____________ Issued by: ____________ Issue No. 01

Date: __________ Designation: __________ Checked by: __________

Date: ____________ Revision No. ____________

CHECK LIST FOR CLEANING IT CHEN EQUIPMENTS AND AREAS DISHWASHING MACHINE

To Check

1. If the machine is clean and free from corrosion? YES/NO
   Especially wash arms, scrap trays and final rinse Jets.
2. If the temperature of:

Pre Wash Tank	100°-120°F	YES/NO
Wash Tank	155°-170°F	YES/NO
Final Rinse	180°-195°F	YES/NO

3. If the water is changed in all tanks every 2-4 hours? YES/NO
4. If the rinse dry bottle or reservoir is filled or replaced and refilled in necessary? YES/NO
5. If switches for heaters for all tanks and final rinse are turned on? YES/NO
6. If drain valves closed tightly and fill valves are opened? YES/NO
7. If switches for dish machine motors and electronic dispenser are turned on? YES/NO
8. If switches and outside of machine flushed out with hose and washed with solution? YES/NO
9. If switches for dish machine motors and electronic dispenser are turned on? YES/NO

Borilers

To Check and Ensure

10. If the entire exteriors, areas underneath and behind the equipment are cleaned? YES/NO
11. If Drip Pans, Racks etc. are soaked in grease cutter solution scrubbed, rinsed and dipped mikrochlor solution and air dried? YES/NO

Overs

To Check

12. If the interior is soaked in grease cutter solution brushed with stiff brush, scraped when necessary and rinsed with clear water and air dried? YES/NO
13. If metal flour inserts when they become stained are

immersed in solution of absorbit in 180°F water brushed with stiff brush and rinsed in clear water? YES/NO

14. If the container used for containing absorbit solution is other than aluminium container? YES/NO
15. If the entire exterior, area underneath and behind the ovens are cleaned? YES/NO

Griddles and Grills

To Check

16. If the base of the griddle the top and sides of the stand the back plate and the spatter shield edges and sides of griddle are thoroughly cleaned? YES/NO
17. If the griddle is brushed with food grade vegetable oil? YES/NO

Steam Jacketed Kettles

To Check

18. If there is any cooked food particles left in the drain channel between the faucet and the outlet of the kettle? YES/NO

Deep Fryer

To Check

19. If there is no warping of the metal of the fryer? YES/NO
20. If the deposits are washed away by using the cleaning solution? YES/NO
21. If the area under, behind and sides are thoroughly cleaned? YES/NO

Steam Tables's

To Check

22. If the top, backboard, front and sides are brush washed with solution of fairy liquid and baked on stubborn food are removed? YES/NO
23. If the time scale is removed from steam walls? YES/NO

Range Hoods and Filters

To Check

24. If the surfaces, outside of inside of hoods and the drain trough are cleaned with grease cutter solution? YES/NO
25. If the channels which hold the filters are cleaned? YES/NO

26. If the exterior surfaces is polished with stainless steel Polish? YES/NO
27. Degreasing once a week is carried out? YES/NO
28. If filters are free from grease? YES/NO

Toasters

To Check and Ensure

29. That electric parts heat elements etc. are not wetted? (as this could cause damage to the toasters or serious injury to personnel when toasters is again plugged on) YES/NO
30. If popup toasters is free from crumbs and the crumb tray is cleaned with fairy liquid solution rinsed and dried with Clean cloth? YES/NO
31. If the counter surfaces underneath the toaster is cleaned? YES/NO
32. If the exterior surface is polished with s/s polish with dry cloth? (to be warned not to get any of the solution inside the toaster) YES/NO

Food Chopper

To Check

33. If the brush with long handle is used for cleaning? YES/NO
34. If all parts are washed in hot fairy liquid solution and thoroughly rinsed with clear water and dipped in sanitizing solution? YES/NO
35. If stationery components are wiped clean with solution of fairy liquid and dried with clean cloth? YES/NO

Blender

To Check

36. If the cup, lid and blade assembly are washed in fairy liquid solution and submerged in solution and air dried? YES/NO
37. If the base of the blender is wiped with fairy liquid solution and cleaned with dry cloth? YES/NO

Meat Mincer

To Check

38. If the electric connection is removed while cleaning?YES/NO
39. If the over and cutter roll assembly are free from meat scraps and they are scrubbed in hot solution of fairy liquid soap? YES/NO

40. If they are rinsed with clear water and sanitized by dipping in solution and air dried? YES/NO
41. If all stationery parts are wiped clean with warm solution? YES/NO

Wet Grinder

42. If the paddle and grinding stone are remove, washed in solution of fairy liquid in hot water, thoroughly rinsed in clear water dipped in solution and air dried? YES/NO
43. If the stationery part is wiped with fairy liquid solution, rinsed in clean water, wiped in solution and air sried? YES/NO

Potato Peeler

To Check

44. If the electric connection is removed and if the lid abrasive disc. Perforated strainer and stopper are flushed with cold water and washed in hot solution of fairy liquid soap? YES/NO
45. If the inside and outside surfaces of stationery are washed in the solution of fairy liquid and brushed with a long handle brush? YES/NO
46. If all parts after washing are rinsed with clear water and again sanitized by rinsing with solution? YES/NO

Meat and Food Slicer

To Check

47. If electric cord is disconnected and blade set at "O"?YES/NO
48. If the blade guard, shafts and all parts under the frame are washed in hot solution of fairy liquid in the sink and rinsed in clear water? YES/NO
49. If all removable parts are dipped in a solution and put in warm water? YES/NO
50. If the stationery parts are cleaned in the positions in solution and scrubbed with a long handle brush? YES/NO

Proof Cabinet

To Check

51. If the cabinet is emptied and the interior and exterior steamed thoroughly? YES/NO

52. If the interior and exterior sprayed with solution and air dried? YES/NO

Stainless Steel Shelving-Counters and Tables

To Check

53. If the table top shelf top and counter top and legs all around cleaned with fairy liquid soap, rinsed with hot clear water, sanitized with solution and air dried? YES/NO

Coffee Maker

To Check

54. If cover, brewing changer container and coffee container are removed to the sink for cleaning hotel solution of fairy liquid soap? YES/NO
55. If the brew reservoir, ports and gauges are a scrubbed with fairy liquid soap solution? YES/NO
56. If the trace of all cleaning solution on these parts is removed completely. YES/NO
57. If the exterior is wiped with fairy liquid soap and wiped dry with clean and try cloth? YES/NO

URN Coffee

To Check

58. If the sides of the interior are brushed with brush pouring clean hot water in to the urn, the hot water after brushing is drained? YES/NO
59. If the interiors sides are again rinsed with hot water drained? YES/NO
60. If the exterior is sprayed with fairy liquid soap and wiped dry with clean dry cloth? YES/NO
61. To check weekly if the decaling is done by bringing the temperature of 160°F the water with lime away filled in the water jacket to just above the scale line allowed to remain in the jacket for one to two hours? YES/NO
62. To check if the water jacket is brushed while draining to remove the softened scale and then rinsed thoroughly with clear water? YES/NO

Coffee Maker-Glass Type

To Check

63. If all units are washed in solution of fairy liquid soap and rinsed in clear water? YES/NO

Pot and Pans Washing

To Check

64. If all excess soil are scraped from pots and pans before they are put into sink for washing? YES/NO
65. To check if 3 steps cleaning, rinsing and sanitizing methods followed? YES/NO

All Sinks (Tanks) and Baskets

To Check

66. If all sinks, baskets, drain boards are washed with brush inside and outside in fairy liquid soap solution? YES/NO
67. If a warm solution of lime-a-way is used for removing the film of mineral deposited, inside sink, baskets and on drain boards? YES/NO

Silverware Burnishing

To Check

68. If silverware are deternishe before burnishing? YES/NO
69. If the grouping of silverware is done i.e. burnishing of forks together knives together spoons together is done? YES/NO
70. If the burnishing solution level is just over the burnishing shots? YES/NO
71. If the silverware pieces do not exceed the recommended number at one time in the burnisher? YES/NO
72. If the burnishing solution is changed every 6 to 7 cycles? YES/NO

Detarnishing Silverware

To Check

73. If aluminium foil sheet is submerged so as to cover completely the bottom of the mobile sink? YES/NO
74. If all silverware are placed into the solution at top of the aluminium foil for 5 to 20 minutes prior to washing? YES/NO

Ice Making Machine

To Check

75. If all parts of the machines inside and outside are brush washed using nylon bristled brush in lime-a way solution? YES/NO
76. If holes in water control are completely cleaned? YES/NO
77. If the parts are rinsed thoroughly with solution? YES/NO
78. If the exterior surface are cleaned with warm solution of fairy liquid soap, rinsed with clean water wiped dry? YES/NO
79. If the exterior S/S surface are polished with S/S polish and wipe dry? YES/NO

Coffee and Tea Dispensers

To Check

80. If all parts are scrub washed with warm solution of Mikrochlor? YES/NO
81. If the facet is carefully dismantled and cleaned in solution? YES/NO

Walk Inreferigerat and Freezers

To Check

82. If the floor is clear of spilled liquid or any food deposit ?And is moped with warm solution? YES/NO
83. If the freezer floor is not mopped with damp mop? YES/NO
84. If during the weekly thorough cleaning all contents are removed to protected storage and ceilings, floors, shelves, braces, hooks, walls are scrubbed with warm fairy liquid soap solution and stubbed soil removed? Then rinsed with clear water? YES/NO
85. If the temperature control of freezer is adjusted to 32°F while cleaning? YES/NO
86. If the sanitization is done by saturating the entire floor surface shelves, walls ceiling with warm solution and air dried ? YES/NO
87. If all contents are put back into refrigerators and freezers and temperature controls are adjusted to normal setting? YES/NO

Reach in Refrierators and Freezers

To Check

88. Of during the weekly thorough cleaning. All shelving's and loose equipments are washed in hot solution of fairly liquid soap rinsed in clean water and sanitized in solution? Then Air dry YES/NO
89. If interior surface especially floor of the box, corner, doors, gasket, handles, latches, ceiling of the box are washed with warm solution Mikro. YES/NO
90. If the interior is sanitized and air dried? YES/NO
91. If the interior is washed with fairy liquid soap and in clean water? Then wiped dry with clean cloth? YES/NO
92. If the exterior s/s or aluminium surfaces are polished with s/stainstentee polish and cleaner? YES/NO

Food Carts

To Check

93. If corners, under shelves, brackets seams and joints are cleaned with dry cloth and sprayed with solution. YES/NO

S/S Carts–Deliming

To Check

94. If lime-a-way solution is applied to the area with water sports, streaks and lime haze and soaked until they are removed? Rinsed with clean water and wiped dry? YES/NO

Can Operners

To Check

95. If shank assembly especially blade and holding mechanism are scrubbed with a stiff bristled brush in to solution of fairy liquid soap? YES/NO
96. If all the parts are rinsed with clean water and sanitized in Mikrochlor solution ? YES/NO
97. If the base is scrubbed with solution and after drying the slot is lubricated? YES/NO
98. If the base is removed from the table, both washed with fairy liquid solution and sanitized in solution then air dried forthrightly? YES/NO

Meat Blocked Sandwich Board, Work Benches Plastic Cutting Boards, Salad Bowls

To Check

99. If all the above articles are wet with warm water? And scrubbed with stiff bristled brush dipped frequently in warm water until all powder is dissolved? YES/NO
100. If these are rinsed with clean warm water and air dried? YES/NO

Garbage Cans, Buckerts and Disposal Containers

To Check

101. If these articles are washed with hot water hose and steam hose after? Then rinsed with solution and air dried? YES/NO
102. Weekly if they are brushed washed with hot solution of absorb it? Spray rinse with clean water and dried? YES/NO

Counter Scales

To Check

103. If scoops or pan and removable parts washed in the pot sink in solution and warm water? YES/NO
104. If stationery surfaces are sprayed by solution and rinsed with clean water and wiped with dry clean cloth? YES/NO

Walls–Tiles, Block and Plaster

To Check

105. If wall tiles, blocks and plaster are cleaned with fairy liquid soap solution? Especially areas subjects to contact with hands such as around light switches and areas above sinks area around key holes, areas just above floor? YES/NO

Stainless Steel Item

To Check

106. If all areas covered by s/s sheet are polished with s/s polished cleaner? YES/NO

Floor of Kitchen Areas

To Check

107. If all floor areas are mopped with fairy liquid frequently? YES/NO
108. If the all fairy solution in the Mopping Bails is frequently changed? YES/NO

CHECK LIST FOR PERSONAL HYGIENE AND GENERAL CLEANLINES

Personal Hygiene

Is it ensured that the kitchen stewarding personnel have.

1. Changed their uniforms before they go on duty? Worn clean shoe? YES/NO
2. Their finger nails trimmed and cleaned? YES/NO
3. Washed their hands and arm with soap and warm water before they go on duty? YES/NO
4. Not been in possession of tobacco in any form beatle leaves. Nuts and chunaa? YES/NO
5. 5 Been warned not to spit in the kitchen area? YES/NO
6. Cut short their hair and shaved their faces? YES/NO
7. Been warmed to wash their hands with soap and warm water each visit to the toilet? YES/NO
8. Been warmed to change their uniform which become badly wet or dirty during the operation? YES/NO
9. Been warmed not to handle any container container containing any kind of under any circumstances? YES/NO

General Cleanliness

Is it Ensured That

1. Ice is kept in clean and closed containers? YES/NO
2. The ice machine and its area cleaned at frequent intervals? YES/NO
3. The ice cubes are transferred into the containers with scoop? YES/NO
4. The cleaned utensils are provided with at all time for storage of food stuff? YES/NO
5. The empty food containers are stored on clean surface above 6" from the ground? YES/NO
6. The surface of kitchen equipments and utensils with which food come in contact, are smooth, clean and with out, clean and without cracks, pits, open seam corrosion and are not chipped off ? YES/NO
7. The Bins, Shelves and containers are cleaned before they are filled in? YES/NO
8. The spaces between fixtures, behind and under table, shelves

under fixture, cutting boards, silcers, choppers, meat saws grinders and peelers are free food particles and dirts? YES/NO

9. The detergents used are checked from time to achieve the desired results? YES/NO
10. The pre washing tank water is changed frequently? YES/NO
11. The dishwashing detergents are added frequently? YES/NO
12. There are sufficient air circulations for quick drying of glasses china and silverware? YES/NO
13. The hot running water are available in all sinks? YES/NO
14. The chipped, cracked china and glassware are discarded? YES/NO
15. The single services item i.e. disposable wares are discarded YES/NO
16. The exhaust fans for steam kettles, ranges, broilers, deepfat fryers ovens etc. are in proper working condition. YES/NO
17. The butchers shop is thoroughly washed and steam cleaned regularly? YES/NO
18. The sinks for posts and pans and the area around are thoroughly washed regularly? YES/NO
19. The door gaskets of refrigerators and freezers are checked for their proper functioning? YES/NO
20. Area cleaning area equipments and detergents are insufficient supply and properly stored? YES/NO
21. The floors are cleaned frequently? YES/NO
22. The ceilings are cleaned along with walls? YES/NO
23. The walls, floors and ceilings are free from holes, cracks and crevices? YES/NO
24. The ceilings are free from openings around pipes, cables and ceilings doors? YES/NO
25. The floor drains are in working order? YES/NO
26. The Bulbs and Lights fixtures are free from grease? YES/NO
27. The Bulbs and Tube lights are in working order? YES/NO
28. The Bulbs and Tube light are having covers? YES/NO
29. The Window and door glass panes are cleaned? YES/NO
30. The reach in and walk in refrigerators and freezer are free from odours? YES/NO
31. The food stuffs kept in the above are free from contamination

ie cooked food are separated from food and all containers are covered and kept above 6" from the floor? YES/NO

32. The meat hooks are clean, smoothand free from pits and rust? YES/NO
33. The engineers are intimated immediately whenever the thermometers of all refrigerators and freezers show undesirable temperatures? YES/NO
34. The flies, cockroaches, other insects and rates are eliminated from all kitchen areas? YES/NO
35. The garbage wet and dry. Are kept in their proper receptacles and cover at all times? YES/NO
36. The garbage cans are emptied and cleaned thrice a day? YES/NO
37. The garbage cans and bags are free from leakage? YES/NO
38. The garbage room is steam cleaned frequently and free from odor? YES/NO
39. The garbage room is refrigerated properly at all times when the filled garbage cans are kept or not inside? YES/NO
40. The garbage room is free from flies, cockroaches, rats and other insects? YES/NO
41. The containers of chemical, poisonous and toxic materials are clearly marked for easy identification? YES/NO
42. The above materials are kept in the away from all kitchens area? YES/NO
43. The chemical used for pest control have distinctive colour so that they cannot be mistaken for food? YES/NO

FORMATS

1. Par Stock–Format

Department________________________ Subject: Chinaware

SL. No. Item	Cover Restaurant LAYOUT	Cover Side STATION	Kitchen Requirement	Restaurant Turn Over	TOTAL
1. Dinner Plate 11					
2. Dinner Plate 10					
3. Dessert Plate 8					
4. B&b Plate 7					
5. Tea Saucer					
6. Tea Cup					
7. Coffee Saucer					
8. Coffee Cup					
9. Soup Cup					
10. Monkey Dish					
11. Nappy Bowl					
12. Ashtray					

FORMATS

2. Inventory

SL. No. Item	Opening Par Stock	Monthly Con-sumption	Yearly Con-sumption	TOTAL	Stock in Control	Store Stock	TOTAL
1. Dinner Plate 11							
2. Dinner Plate 10							
3. Dessert Plate 8							
4. B&b Plate 7							
5. Tea Saucer							
6. Tea Cup							
7. Coffee Saucer							
8. Coffee Cup							
9. Soup Cup							
10. Monkey Dish							
11. Nappy Bowl							
12. Ashtray							
13. Ashtray							
14. Fish Plate							
Total Opera-tional Budget							

Format

Subject: Chinaware.

BREAKAGE AND DISCARD REPORT FORMAT

Department______________________________No. 0001

SL. No.	*Item Code*	*Item Description*	*Unit*	*Qty*	*Unit Price*	*Amount*	*Remarks*

Prepared by	Department Head	Verified by	Approved by	

INVENTORY CONTROL

Food Store					
Beverage Store					
General Store					
Housekeeping Store					
Engineering Store					

1. Purchase Indents are raised by Department Head for Non-Inventory Item.
2. Capital Goods Requirements as Budget.
3. Addition Capital Authorisation for Unplanned Capital Requirements.
4. Purchase Requisition are Raised by inventory controller for all purchase.
5. Inventory levels are fixed taking into consideration lead time and monthly consumption.
6. PR's are made on monthly and weekly basis as per the ABC analysis I.E. Frequent orders for high value/ Consumption items and monthly order for low value items.
7. On Receipt of goods in stores. There are checked with Drr and Entered in the System.
8. An SRC is checked for every item received.
9. Item are checked and stacked.
10. Issues are made against authorized requisition by Respective Department Heads.
11. Issue are done on first out basis.

INVENTORY MANAGEMENT

Objectives

1. Minimise Investment.
2. To meet demand of Operations.

Cost

Ordering Cost
Carrying Cost

1. **Storage**
   Insurance

Deterioration
Serving

2. **Opportunity Cost**
Management Techniques

Management Techniques

- ABC Analysis
- Economic order Quantity
- Re-order Point
- Safety Stock

Working Capital Management

"Working Capital" refers to funds invested in current assets.

"Net Working" is the difference between the current assets and current liabilities.

Working capital management policies have a great influence on the company's.

- Profitability.
- Liquidity.
- Structural Health.
- Working capital should neither be excess nor inadequate.
- Excess working capital would indicate company has idle liabilities.
- Paucity of working capital may lead to inability in meeting liabilities.

Current ratio is considered along with acid test ratio to be the indicator of working capital situation.

Cash Debtors Operational Stores other stores.

Factors Determining the Requirements of working capital are:

- Credit Policies
- Inventory Policies
- Credit Worthiness.

EXAMPLES OF KITCHEN STEWARDING FORMATS

Capital Budget Requirement for the year 2009-10

		Capital Budget Requirement for the year 2009-10				
		Department– Kitchen Stewarding				
S.No.	*Items*	*Specification*	*Qty.*	*Apprx. Cost*	*Amount*	*Justification*
	F&B Production Banquet Kitchen					
1.	S. Steel Kadahi	16", 304, 10g	2	2500	5000	Required for Live Counters
2.	S. Steel Kadahi	20", 304, 10g	2	3500	7000	Required for Live Counters
3	S. Steel Tawa	24", 304, 10g	2	2400	4800	Required for Live Counters
4.	S. Steel Tawa	28", 304,10g	2	2850	5700	Required for Live Counters
5.	S. Steel Rice Stainer	20", 304, 12g	4	3250	13000	Required for Live Counters
6.	S. Steel Rice Stainer	24", 304, 12G	2	4500	9000	Required for Live Counters
7.	S. Steel Stand for Rice	30"	10	3280	32800	Required for Live Counters
8.	S. Steel Deep Fryer	Portable	2	7000	14000	Required for Live Counters
9.	S. Steel Cane Opner Table Mounted	Imported	2	4000	8000	Stand by
10.	S. Steel Jalebi Tawi	16" 304, 10 G	2	2850	5700	Required for Live Counters
11.	Qureshi Pan		2	3200	6400	Required for Live Counters
12.	Brass Patila with LID	28", 10G, with Kalai	4	10500	42000	Existing about to be Discarded

13.	Brass Patila with LID	26" 10G, with Kalai	6	8500	51000	Required More
14.	Brass Patila with LID	24", 10G, with Kalai	4	7500	30000	Required More
15.	Mixie	Branded	10	3000	30000	For all Kitchens
16.	Vegetable Juicer	Imported	1	18500	18500	For Coffee Shop
17.	S. Steel Juicer	Imported	1	13500	13500	For Coffee Shop
18.	Vegetable Basket	60 LTR, Green	18	1150	20700	For all Kitchens
19.	Vegetable Basket	48 LTR, Yellow	6	650	3900	For Banquet Kitchen
20.	Vegetable Basket	48 LTR, Blue	4	650	2600	For Banquet Kitchen
21.	Vegetable Basket	48 LTR, Red	6	650	3900	For Banquet Kitchen
22.	Tod Box	48 LTR, Yellow	6	650	3900	For Banquet Kitchen
23.	Tupper Ware Jars	Assorted, 1KG, 2KG		200000	200000	For All Kitchens & Bakery
	For Dry Item	5KG,10KG,				For All Kitchens & Bakery
24.	Cambro Poly-Carbonate	Assorted Sizes		200000	200000	For All Kitchens & Bakery
	Food Storage Boxes					
				Total	**731400**	
	Kitchen Stewarding					
1.	S. Steel Garbage Trolley	30"HT×42 "L×28"WD	1	20000	20000	We have 2 Required 1 more
2.	S. Steel Hot Plate	30"L×18"WD ×12"HT	2	10000	20000	We have 2 Required 2 more
3.	S. Steel Round Food Pan	Same as Existing	18	1500	27000	Required More
4.	Ceramic Round Food	Same as Existing	18	2000	36000	Required More
5.	Pressure Washer	Kacher	1	45000	45000	To Maintain high Level of Cleaning

6.	S. Steel Tea URN 25LTR		2	1850	3700	For tea Service at Aanpoorna
7.	S. Steel Tea URN 5LTR		2	1250	2500	For tea Service at Aanpoorna
8.	Garbage Drums S. Steel On Wheels	Same as Existing	12	2500	30000	24 NOS we have Required More In Operations
9.	S. S. Trolley (Wheel Base) For Garbage Drums		24	500	12000	To Carry Garbage Drums
10.	Sigri for Pool Side	M S, 36"HT	20	1200	24000	Existing about to be Discarded
11.	Clay Tandoor Insert		12	3500	42000	For Banquets, Tapas, & Paatra
12.	Refrigerator Cabine	100 LTR Branded	1	35000	35000	For Cafetaria
13.	S. Steel Racks	6'x3' with 5 Selves With Lock & Key	3	15000	30000	2 for Cafetaria Dry Store 1 for Eggs Back Area to Kept Buffet Equipments
14.	Buffet Props for Display				200000	For Buffet Up Gradation
				Total	**527200**	
	F&B SERVICE BANQUETS					
1.	SS Roll top Chaffing Dishes	12 LTR, Rect Imported	24	9500	228000	24 NOS old Chaffing Dishes about to be Discarded
2.	Wooden Bowls for Buffet Display with Glass Top	Set of three 30", 24" 18"	3 sets	12000 Set	36000	For Buffet Display
3.	Brass Handi with Sigri		12 sets	10000	120000	For VIP Parties
4.	Snacks Warmer	As per Sample	20	2000	40000	For VIP Parties
5.	Buffet Tables			300000	300000	For Upgradation

6.	ICE Cream Display Cabinet	AMS Scoopy ICE 2	2	94000	188000	For Buffet Display
7.	Moblie Esspresso Coffee	Branded	1	45000	45000	Coffee Service at Pool side Parties Machine
8.	Garland Stand S. Steel	As per sample	2	10000	20000	We do not have
9.	Folding Stage on wheels		12	25000	300000	We do not have, Hierd from out side
10.	Bar Trolley		2	25000	50000	We do not have, for Upgradation
11.	ICE Cabinet	50LTR, Cambro	2	32000	64000	We do not have,
				Total	**1391000**	
	COFFEE SHOP					
1.	Juice Dispencer	10 LTR, Imported	2	7000	14000	Replacement
2.	Cereal Dispencer	Triple Jars, Impted	1	18000	18000	Replacement
3.	Buffet Tables	Wooden	4	25000	100000	For Eggs Buffet Display
4.	Milk Boiler	5 LTR, Imported	1	14000	14000	For Eggs Buffet Display
5.	Water Boiler	25 LTR, Imported	1	18500	18500	Replacement
6.	Ice Crusher Machine	25 LTR, Imported	1	35000	35000	For Eggs
7.	S. Steel Bar for Milk & Juices	4 Compt, Impted	1	15000	15000	For Eggs Buffet Display
8.	Display Chilling Cabinet With Cover		1	30000	30000	For Salad Display
	Indian Restaurant			**Total**	**244500**	
1	Three Compartment Dish	Copper	12	1000	12000	For Saunf & Mishri Serving
2	Wine Racks	Wooden	1	20000	20000	For Wine Display at Indian Restaurant
	ROOM SERVICE			**Total**	**32000**	

1	S. Steel Tray Jacks	S. Steel	6	2000	12000	Required in R/s for Upradation
				Total	12000	
	CHINESE RESTAURANT					
1	Flambe/ Carving Trolley	Imported	1	30000	30000	For Live Cooking at Chinese Restaurant
				Total	30000	
	Provison for Miscellaneous	ITEMS			250000	
				Grand Total	**3218100**	

EXAMPLES OF KICHEN STEWARDING FORMAT OF CAPITAL BUDGET FOR A YEAR

Capital Stewarding Capital Budget 2008-09

2010-11

S.No.	*Items*	*Qty*	*Rate*	*Amount*	*Specs*	*Remark*
1.	S/S Stock Pot Stove	6	10125	60750	24×24×24 With Drip Tray	Not Required
2.	Canteen Burner with Guard	2	1800	3600		Carry Forward
3.	S/S Griddle with Guard	1	14063	14063	24×18×10	Not Required
4.	Angle Fitted Rack (Dixon Rack)	2	3000	6000	72×36×18	Not Required
5.	ICE Crusher	1	34000	34000	Automatic	Not Required
6.	Plate Warmer	2	26000	52000	1×12×50	Not Required
7.	**Water Boiler**	1	9506	9506	20LTR	Pending
8.	S/S ICE DISPENSER	6	5500	33000		Not Required
9.	**Phulka Puffer with Guard**	2	12938	25876		Pending
10.	**Iron Tandoor Stand**	4	1500	6000		Pending

Note: Item No. 7, 9, 10, has Indented Purchase order has raised these items proc Items might be received in Next Financial Year.

Kitchen Stewarding Capital Budget
2008-09 Budget 2009-10

S.No.	Items	Qty	Rate	Amount	Specs	Remark
1.	Folding state on	10 Blocks	30000	300000	8FT×4FT×18"H One Block Top Fitted with 1/2" PLY On Top Fitted with Carpet 4" Heavy Duty Angle All Around	Required for Bqt Parties Stage Set-up
2.	Buffet Tables For Banquets	24	12500		Designer Table, S/Steel/Wooden Or with Glass Top In three Different Sizes	For Buffet Upgradation
3.	Buffet Props		200000		Imported Glass Vases and other Decorative Items	For Buffet Upgradation
4.	Buffet Tables for Coffee Shop	2 2 2 2	15000 12000 10000 10000	30000 24000 20000 20000 94000	6FT×2T×30" 4FT×2FT×36" 2FT×2FT×40" 18"×18"×36" Made out of Seasoned Barmoh Legs To Fitted with 19MM water Proof Board with Lamination	Required for Brunch Buffet Upgradation
5.	Tupper Ware	24 24			1KG 2 KG	Required For Storage in

Contd...

S.No.	Items	Qty	Rate	Amount	Specs	Remark
		24			5KG	Dry Stores at
		12			10KG	Restaurat
		12			15 KG	Banquet Kitchen
		12			20 KG	and Bakery
6.	Polycarbonate	18	1000	18000	12183CW	Required for
	Containers	18	1200	21600	12186CW	Storage in Cold
		12	1500	18000	12189CW	Rooms & Deep
		12	3000	36000	18269CW	Freezers
		12	2400	28800	18266CW	At Indian
		12			1×1	Restaurat,
		12			1×2	Cofee Shop,
		12			1×4	Banquet Kitchen
		12			1×6	and Bakery
		12			1×9	
		Apprx Cost		200000		
7.	Miscellaneous			250000	Contingency for Kitchen Equipments & Buffet Display	

Chemicals and Cleaning Items for all the Kitchen Stewarding Areas

S. No.	*Item*	*April*	*May*	*June*
1.	NYLON BRUSH 18"			
2.	GARBAGE BAG GREEN			
3.	GARBAGE BAG RED			
4.	GARBAGE BAG YELLOW			
5.	SCOTCH BRITE			
6.	SUMA GRILL 5 LTR CAN D-9			
7.	SUMA DET 5 LTR CAN-D1			
8.	SUMA DIP 5 LTR CAN			
9.	SUMA BREAK UP			
10.	SUMA SILVER 5 LTR CAN D-8			
11.	SUMA SCALE 5 LTR CAN D-5			
12.	SUMA TAB 900 GMS BTL			
13.	STRIDE (FLOOR CLEANER)			
14.	LIQUID SOAP–Lever plus			
15.	SOFT HAND CARE GEL 500ML BTL			
16.	VIM POWDER 1KG PKT			
17.	SUMA MULTI 5 LTR CAN D2.3L			
18.	BROOM HARD			

Contd...

S. No.	Item	April	May	June
19.	BROOM SOFT			
20.	MOP DRY FRAME ONLY			
21.	MOP REFIL			
22.	SPONG WITH SCOTCH BRITE			
23.	SQEEZER WITH HANDLE			
24.	SWIPE & SHINE 3M			
25.	UTILITY KITCHEN ROLL 290057			
26.	CAPS DISPOSABLE			
27.	GLOVES SERGICAL			
28.	GLOVES DISPOSABLE			
29.	SUMA DRAIN			
30.	DUST PAN G.1			
31.	C-FOLD SMALL			

Equipments for HACCP Stations

1.	HAND WASH SINK
2.	PADDIE OPERATED DUSTBIN
3.	DISPENCER FOR C-FOLD NAOKINS
4.	PLUNGER FOR HAND WASH GEL
5.	KENTUCKY MOP TROLLEY

SALE OF BURNT OIL VS. F&B SALE FOR 2008-09
KITCHEN STEWARDING 2009-10

Month	*Selling Rate*	*Quantity Sold*	*Amount*	*F&B Sale*	*% OF Sale*	*TOTAL Cover*	*% OF Cover*	*Amount Per Cover*	*Discard Per Day*	*Amount Per Day*
APRIL										
MAY										
JUNE										
JULY										
AUGUST										
SEPTEMBER										
OCTOBER										
NOVEMBER										
DECEMBER										
JANUARY										
FEBRUARY										
MARCH										

KITCHEN STEWARDING
SALE OF BURNT OIL VS. F&B SALE FOR 2008-09

Month	Selling Rate	Quantity Sold	Amount	F&B Sale	% OF Sale	TOTAL Cover	% OF Cover	Amount Per Cover	Discard Per Day	Amount Per Day
APRIL	18									
MAY	18									
JUNE	18									
JULY	18									
AUGUST	18									
SEPTEMBER	18									
OCTOBER	18									
NOVEMBER	18									
DECEMBER	18									
JANUARY	18									
FEBRUARY	18									
MARCH	18									
Grand Total										

NOTE: BUYING RATE = RS45/ PER LTR

Index